Flight From Prague

The Making of a Refugee

Michael Lewis

Flight From Prague

The Making of a Refugee
September 1938 – November 1939

Michael Lewis

Haythorp Books

First published by Haythorp Books 2025
This edition published 2025

Haythorp Books, a division of Canbury Press Kingston upon Thames, Surrey, United Kingdom
www.canburypress.com

Typeset in Athelas (heading), Futura PT (body)

Cover: Catherine Trehy

All rights reserved © Michael Lewis

Michael Lewis has asserted his right to be identified as the author of this work in accordance with Section 77 of the Copyright, Designs and Patents Act 1988

This is a work of non-fiction

ISBN:
Paperback: 9781914487552
Ebook: 9781914487569

Contents

Notes on Sources	7
1. Prelude	9
2. Limbo	33
3. Adrift	79
4. Transit	103
5. Alien	131
6. Re-united	169
7. New World	177
8. What Happened Next	193
Afterword	*197*
Notes	*199*
Acknowledgements	*217*
A Linen Handkerchief	*221*
Michael Lewis	*222*

NOTES ON SOURCES

The detailed re-construction of thirteen months in the life of Harry Lewy presents some obvious challenges: the events chronicled in this story occurred nearly 90 years ago, the protagonist himself died in 1991.

I have, however, been able to rely on a number of primary and secondary sources.

The stories families tell and pass from generation to generation provided the starting point. Between us, my brother, Robin and myself, pieced together the many conversations we had with our parents over decades to lay the foundations of Harry's story. Occasionally, detail varied but they are the solid bedrock of this story.

Contemporary documents in our possession which somehow survived the turmoil of the times complement the family stories. These are limited but crucial and include entries in Max's passport, employment references from the 1930s, a statement from the Nazi police that Harry did not have a police record and his residence permit in Czechoslovakia. I have had sight of documents about Harry held by the National Archives at Kew, the Public Record Office of Northern Ireland (PRONI) and the Czech State Archives in Trutnov, formerly Trautenau.

An extensive and still growing literature exists about this period. It covers analysis of the politics of Appeasement and its consequences, the ill-fated history of Czechoslovakia, the troubled relationship between Czechs, Germans and Jews, and the British Government's response to refugees from Nazism. It also includes contemporary reports and newspaper accounts and eye-witness memoirs of the *Anschluss*, the Nazi annexation of Austria, and the *Reichspogromnacht* of 9 November 1938, also known as *Kristallnacht*. I had read widely in this area, long before the story was conceived.

Unlike today, there were no smart phones or electronic devices to record every word, image, move and thought. Where the narrative demanded, I have therefore dramatised certain conversations and episodes, based on the combined sources outlined above. Taken together they re-construct Harry Lewy's life-changing experience of becoming a refugee.

And a note on names

The Sudetenland was predominantly German-speaking until the expulsion of the German population after the end of World War Two. After the creation of Czechoslovakia in 1918 the region was officially bi-lingual. Today, the towns and cities of the region are known only by their Czech names. I have largely used the German names with which Harry would have been familiar, thus, his birth place is Trautenau, today Trutnov, he worked in Reichenberg, today Liberec and his university friend came from Eger, today Cheb. I have retained the Czech names of Dvůr Králové and Pardubice rather than Königinhof and Pardubitz to mark the difference between those places ceded to Germany after the Munich agreement and those which remained, however briefly, part of Czechoslovakia. Both languages were used widely in the capital, for which I have used the English name, Prague, in preference to Prag or Praha.

1.
PRELUDE

Reichenberg, Czechoslovakia, 30 September 1938

"Herr Doktor, it really is time to leave!"

Ignaz, agitated, stood in the office doorway, shifting from foot to foot.

"There's no time to waste! It's turning ugly. It'll be dark in an hour or so. You can't stay here a minute longer."

Dr Leon Harry Lewy, 29, unmarried, of average height, slightly over-weight, and with already greying, thinning hair, said nothing. Pensive, distracted, uncertain at first how to respond to Ignaz' insistence, he contemplated the habitual items of his daily work in charge of textile imports and exports, lying scattered in front of him across his imposing mahogany desk.

"So it's come to this," he muttered. Gazing at the wooden calendar on his desk he realised he had forgotten to roll forward the date. He twiddled Thursday into Friday 30 September 1938, staring at the red numbers. What would the day's events in Munich mean?

Had Mister Chamberlain and Monsieur Daladier really given in? He glanced in the direction of Ignaz at the office door, adding with bitterness in his voice, "so, the Sudetens are going *'Heim ins Reich'* after all."

The slogan, endlessly trumpeted through the streets of the Sudetenland in recent times had finally become reality. At the stroke of a pen everything in his orderly world had become uncertain. There would be no home for him in that Reich; of that, at least, he was sure.

"Please, Herr Doktor," pleaded Ignaz, interrupting Harry's thoughts, "you need to get away from Reichenberg straight away!"

UNITED AND SECURE: *The Lewy Family: Minna, Arthur, Harry, Max, ca 1921*

Trautenau, Czechoslovakia, Sunday 25 September 1938

"*Gut yom tov*," Harry proclaimed to announce his arrival as he opened the heavy front door to the family home.

Home lay in Trautenau, a small, picturesque, industrial town in north-east Bohemia, nestling at the foot of the Giant Mountains. On the Sunday of that week he had travelled 90 kilometres or so east of Reichenberg to his parents to celebrate the beginning that evening of *Rosh Hashanah*, the New Year, as he had done every year since returning from his studies abroad in Florence six years previously. He enjoyed the freedom of living in Reichenberg, a lively provincial town with a thriving cultural and social life. It was close enough for him to see his parents every few weeks but at the same time far enough from Trautenau to allow him to pursue his own private bachelor's existence.

The Lewy family processed solemnly the short distance along Reichstrasse, crossed the bridge over the Aupa and turned left and gently uphill to the synagogue on Rinnelstrasse. As the occasion demanded, they were dressed in their best clothes, the epitome of a solidly bourgeois, respectable, prosperous family. His mother looked graceful and dignified, Harry thought, while his father cut a stately figure. Arthur, his younger brother, once again out of town, would miss spending the New Year at home.

"Let's hope Arthur will be home next week for *Yom Kippur*," Harry said quietly to his father.

"Yes, let's hope," his father replied as they entered the synagogue. "It would be good for the whole family to be together for a day or two." Harry nodded in agreement.

"I'd like that," added his mother, "we see him so rarely these days."

Harry wore his religious observance increasingly lightly. Partly out of respect for his parents, partly from habit, he made a point of spending the High Holy Days at home but that was now as far as the discharge of his religious obligations went. Ever since leaving home, first to study briefly in Paris, then for three years in Vienna at the *Hochschule für Welthandel*, the University College for International Trade, and subsequently in Florence to complete his doctorate, the ardour with which he practised his Judaism had gradually diminished. Nonetheless, the intimacy of the family and the excellent food his mother prepared on festive occasions easily enticed him back to Trautenau. He enjoyed being there and it was also an opportunity to catch up with the few old friends who still remained in the town of his birth. There was nothing dutiful about spending the New Year at home.

The service that day seemed interminable. Harry was not the only member of the congregation distracted by events unfolding at bewildering speed around them. The men gathered in front of the building at the end of the morning service. The synagogue exuded the community's erstwhile confident sense of permanence. Their conversation that morning, normally so animated, boisterous even, was muted. Wishes for a Happy New Year sounded more like a question than an affirmation. What would this new year bring? News was exchanged but the usual small-town gossip was missing. Instead the conversation turned on who had already left the country, who was planning to go and where to? Everyone knew an acquaintance, a relative or friend from just across the border in Germany or in Austria, who had told them how precarious life had become. For some standing in quiet huddles, Palestine was a possibility, for others the United States, England or even Argentina. A few, but only a few, dismissed out of hand the notion of abandoning a homeland where they lived so comfortably. Czechoslovakia, they told themselves, was not Germany but an independent, democratic republic with powerful friends to east and west.

The little congregation dispersed. Harry rejoined his parents for the short walk home where a ceremonial meal would be waiting. Reichsstrasse 25, the family home, the only home Harry had ever known, was an unostentatious but nonetheless impressive stone-fronted building on a pleasant tree-lined street leading out of town. It expressed a stolid permanence. Like the synagogue, the house dated from the 1880s, when the burgeoning Jewish communities in the German-speaking areas of Bohemia were growing in confidence and size. The family felt secure and accepted; with apparent good reason they looked forward to a bright future within the complex cultural mosaic which made up the Austro-Hungarian Empire under his imperial and royal majesty, Franz Josef. Or so it had seemed in the years before the Great War.

Later on Monday almost everyone listened to the wireless and heard the menace in Adolf Hitler's speech the previous evening at the *Sportpalast* in Berlin. It contained nothing new. They all knew trouble was coming. After Hitler's closing speech at the annual Nuremberg Nazi Party Rally a fortnight before, there had been a brief outburst of serious disorder in Trautenau and neighbouring towns. Czech families as well as German-speaking Social Democrats had had to flee the town to escape the local Nazis. The Czech authorities had initially been caught off guard as local youths rampaged briefly under the arcades on the market square, chanting and waving flags, occasionally smashing the windows of premises they claimed were owned by Jews. Then a unit of the Czech army had arrived and imposed a temporary peace.

Martial law was still in place in numerous districts elsewhere in the Sudetenland. If the German forces assembling close by on the other side of the border did invade, the worshippers who had gathered in the

Rinnelstrasse knew they would be prime targets. Would the powerful Czech army, widely reputed to be the best equipped and trained in Europe and which had mobilised over the previous weekend, really fight? From right across the republic came reports on the wireless of Czechs demanding resistance.

The mood that morning outside the synagogue had been unusually tense and fearful. Harry had remained silent, lost in sombre thought. Gaps had begun to appear in the normally packed synagogue.. Where was everyone? There had been nothing celebratory in the piercing notes of the *Shofar* which closed the service. This year it had sounded strangely shrill and for Harry chillingly ominous, no longer a portent of triumph but more a warning.

EARNEST YOUNG MAN: *Harry ca 1928, possibly passport photograph*

Prelude

Reichenberg, Friday 30 September 1938

"Thank you, Ignaz, I've just got a couple of letters to finish before the weekend. I won't be long." Harry, chain-smoking, took a new cigarette from his silver case and replied, "and I'd like to make a quick telephone call to Liesl." Despite the calm exterior he presented to the outside world, he knew that in recent months he had been relying increasingly on cigarettes to settle his fraying nerves.

Ignaz Baumann, normally taciturn, invariably courteous, deferential but never obsequious, always aware of his position as the general factotum and caretaker of Beckmann and Steinhauer Textiles Limited, could not conceal his alarm. Old enough to be Harry's father, Ignaz had come to the firm shortly after the Great War following a mining accident. An equally devout Catholic and loyal trade unionist, he had resisted all pressure to join the *Sudetendeutsche Partei* led by the local Nazi leader, Konrad Henlein, as it grew in popularity and strength. Its appeal to a pan-German national identity, an Aryan race, held no attraction for him. The son of a German-speaking Austrian father and a Czech mother, he tended to see matters differently from many of his compatriots. Ignaz was not given to extravagant emotion or gesture nor to speaking out of turn, as he might have seen it, but on this occasion, he did not hold back.

"It's not safe, Herr Doktor!" he insisted. "Come over here! Listen! Can you hear them?"

He opened the office window wider. In the distance Harry could make out a vague rumbling which, as he listened harder, became the unmistakable rhythmic beat of a martial drumming. A chant of "*Juda verrecke!* Judah perish!" echoed in the narrow streets.

"They're preparing a welcome for our German neighbours. It's only a matter of time now. The agreement comes into effect at midnight.

Reichenberg isn't Vienna but you know as well as I do what happened there."

Harry had been shaken by the horrors which followed the *Anschluss*, the Nazi annexation of Austria, earlier in the year. The newspapers had been full of lengthy accounts; the wireless had carried harrowing eye-witness reports but it had been an agonised letter from Trudie which had distressed him most of all. He was still in regular contact with his former girlfriend. She lived with her parents in the heart of the city and described how the Viennese had turned viciously on their Jewish neighbours, her family included. He also knew what had transpired earlier that day in Munich. Everyone had heard the broken and beleaguered government of independent Czechoslovakia broadcast its brow-beaten acceptance of the *diktat* to the distressed citizens of the country.

Harry slipped a few papers into his briefcase, got to his feet, took his coat and fedora hat from the clothes-stand in the corner of the office and indicated to Ignaz that he was ready. The letters and telephone call would have to wait. As he reached the door where Ignaz was waiting for him, Harry picked up a smallish suitcase of the kind a commercial traveller spending a few nights away from home might use. Glancing one last time at his desk, he turned out the light and stepped silently on to the top rung of the fire escape which led down into the yard below.

Trautenau, Sunday 25 September 1938
The *Rosh Hashanah* festive meal had been all that he had expected. As usual his father, Max, had presided, starting with a short blessing. He kept the conversation low key, reminiscing about how over forty years before, as a young adventurer seeking his fortune far from his native

Baltic coast, he had celebrated his first High Holy Days in South Africa in a bell-tent on the edge of a dusty town in the Transvaal.

"I never did find gold and diamonds," he said, smiling.

Then his mother, Minna, had joined in with her own tales of how she and her classmates at her girls' school in Memel, also on the Baltic, observed the New Year and Day of Atonement with solemnity. It was a conversation which over the years had come to occupy a ritual position in the Lewy family's marking of the New Year. Arthur, Harry's younger brother, found it tedious, which perhaps explained his absence on this occasion. By contrast, Harry was amused by its predictability and enjoyed his father's tales of derring-do in Africa, which had become more elaborate with the passing of the years.

Max signalled the end of formalities by opening a box of Havanas which his brother-in-law, Sam, had sent from the United States. He selected one without offering Harry a cigar and carefully lit up. Minna had withdrawn to attend to the coffee.

"So, what does this New Year 5699 hold for us?" This too was a familiar question. Speculation now replaced reminiscence.

Reichenberg, Friday 30 September 1938
Ignaz had taken charge.

"When the lorry enters the yard, Herr Doktor, go straight down the steps and climb into the back. Lie flat and pull the tarpaulin as tightly as you can over yourself and your case. Don't say anything and try not to move."

A multitude of questions tumbled into Harry's mind.

"Where are we going?"

"Away from here. Out of Reichenberg. Out of the Sudetenland into the Czech lands proper, away from the Germans."

"Can I stop off at my flat to collect a few things? It's only a few streets away."

"It's too late for that. There are crowds in the streets. They're planning a torch-light parade. Armed gangs of *Freikorps* have been busy organising. It's too risky. And they have been drinking all day, waiting for their moment of glory."

Harry was momentarily taken aback by Ignaz's assertiveness but accepted his commands. The noise from the town travelled clearly in the cool late September evening.

The wheezing sound of a small lorry announced its arrival and Harry hurried towards it as instructed. A man wearing a worker's flat cap dismounted from the driver's cab and greeted him near the bottom of the fire escape with a familiar smile.

"Good evening, Herr Doktor."

It was Alois, Ignaz's younger brother. Harry knew him well; he was a skilled carpenter and had made some elegant furniture for his bachelor flat. They had struck up a kind of friendship. Harry was relieved to see him.

"Please climb in the back and make yourself as comfortable as you can under the tarpaulin. You'll have a companion. I think you know Herr Doktor Heller."

Harry indeed knew Otto Heller. For a short time they had been good-natured rivals for the attention of Liesl Hamburger, the main attraction of the Reichenberg Maccabi Tennis Club.

"Where are we going?" he asked again.

"To the Czech lands. Königinhof, that's to say Dvůr Králové, or a bit further, Hradec Králové perhaps or even towards Pardubice," came a slightly hesitant reply. "Please remain out of sight until we are well clear of the town."

"Dvůr Králové. Can we call in briefly at my parents in Trautenau? It's on the way."

"No." The reply was emphatic. "It's too dangerous. The Czech Army is on the roads but they are already withdrawing from the towns. The roads are safe for now, they have set up checkpoints but Henlein's people are already in control of all the towns. They're waiting for the *Wehrmacht* to arrive. They're in a wild mood."

Harry understood. He turned to Ignaz, who had followed him down the fire escape into the factory yard and shook his hand, murmuring a brief thank you before clambering compliantly on to the open-backed lorry and finding a space under the tarpaulin.

"May God keep you safe, Doktor Lewy," Ignaz had replied as he disappeared into the gathering darkness.

IN HAPPIER TIMES: Harry, aged 20, poses for the camera with his tennis racket ca 1929

Trautenau, Sunday 25 September 1938

"The way I see things," began Max in his confident tones, enjoying the Havana which concluded dinner, "we are having another of Mr Hitler's tantrums. It will all blow over in a day or two. All bluff and bluster. Nobody in his right mind wants a war."

"Nobody in his right mind," mused Harry silently but he did not interrupt his father's flow.

"The Czechs will have to give Henlein and his crowd a bit more autonomy but that will be it. This *'Heim ins Reich'* nonsense, it's all hot air. We will become a kind of Bohemian Switzerland. Life will go on."

Harry did not feel it was his place to accuse his father of complacency or naivety but he struggled to conceal his disagreement. Instead, he adopted a more cautious approach.

"I'm not quite so sure," he began, "so much has happened. *Anschluss*. The May crisis, for example. A terrible shock. And then the Germans began troop manoeuvres in Saxony, right on the border."

"Yes, but they soon backed down when the Czech army mobilised. All talk, empty rhetoric, if you ask me," interjected his father.

"So, just a tactic," continued Harry, sipping the black coffee his mother had discreetly brought into the dining room.

"Setting the world to rights, are we?" she said gently, placing the tray in front of her husband before slipping out of the room again.

"Our President, Doctor Beneš, has tried and tried again. He has made so many concessions but every time it looks like there is a chance of progress, Henlein ups the ante. Hitler's pulling the strings!"

"I don't think it's as bad as you make out," persisted his father. "Trautenau's not Kishinev, you know. It's not as if the Germans are uncivilised Cossacks. It's not 1903, they're not going to massacre people in the streets."

"For Heaven's sake, what more evidence do you want?" snapped Harry, exasperated. "Look at all the trouble round here just a few weeks ago and in Eger too, and the other towns. The fighting, deaths, martial law; it was a proper insurrection, you know, orchestrated from across the border. And after that, more demonstrations and then last weekend, the Czech army fully mobilised, one million men under arms in twenty-four hours. And you say it's not that bad!"

Harry paused, surprised at his own vehemence.

"I'm sorry," he added, "I didn't mean to be aggressive. It's just that..."

Max cut in. "It's fine, maybe there's something in what you say," he continued, breaking the tension which had followed Harry's outburst.

"It doesn't look good, does it? Still, we'll be all right, though; after all we're British citizens."

Max, almost sixty-four years old, portly, balding and sporting a discreet but distinguished silver moustache, rose slowly from his seat, made his way to the sideboard and desk at the other end of the dining room and took a small booklet out of the top drawer. Summoning up his most authoritative register to bolster his mere five feet and five inches, he began to read, in the manner of a proclamation:

"'By His Britannic Majesty's......'".

Harry could feel his own agitation mounting syllable by syllable....

'request and require in the Name of His Majesty all those whom it may concern to allow the bearer to pass freely without let or hindrance and to afford him every assistance and protection...'

Harry knew the text by heart. His father was immensely proud of the little dark blue document, number 946, bearing the precious words British Passport and beneath the imperial crest United Kingdom of Great Britain and Northern Ireland. Below that, written in turquoise ink in the hand of Captain JW Taylor MBE, his long-standing friend at the Embassy who knew all about what Max had done for the Empire, *Mr Max S LEWY*. Lewy, written in capital letters, was underlined.

Harry no longer contained his frustration.

"And you really think that when our local Nazis kick down the door, they will say 'Oh, we've made a terrible mistake; it's our dear old friend, Mr Lewy and he's such a nice English gentleman. Just look at his lovely passport. We do apologise for disturbing you, sir, we wish you a pleasant evening'. Do you really think that's what will happen? No, they won't see a friend or a fine English gentleman. They'll see what they've always wanted to see. A Jew, an ugly little Jew, desperately clutching a passport!"

A silence fell around the dinner table. Harry instantly regretted his stridency. Had he gone too far? This was not the usual way he addressed his father. At the same time, he felt a brief release from the anxiety which had been gnawing at him for days.

"And what do you suppose will happen to us if the worst happens? To me? What assistance and protection will my Czechoslovak passport offer me? Or Arthur?"

Another protracted silence enveloped the room.

"Maybe you're not completely wrong," Max said, offering a reconciliatory concession.

"It might be a good idea to take a few precautions but still, I do think it will calm down in a few days, it always does."

Harry remained non-committal. He no longer wished to pursue the conversation. Max, used to having the final word, returned to his earlier theme.

"You know, we are not alone in our little republic. England and France are our friends and allies. I know the English, the mighty British Empire. They won't let us down. They are men of honour. Prime Minister Chamberlain will put Reichskanzler Hitler in his place." As an afterthought he added, "and what's more, even the Soviet Union is on our side."

Harry decided it was time for a truce.

"I need to be getting back to Reichenberg. Tomorrow is a normal working day. I'll be home next week for *Kol Nidrei* and *Yom Kippur*. We can talk about all this then and decide what to do, if the worst comes to the worst. We'll have plenty of time. *Yom Kippur* is always a long day."

His father concurred. "Yes, let's do that. It'll all have quietened down by then, you'll see."

Father and son embraced. Harry kissed his mother, who was standing in the hall, lightly on the cheek and was gone. Minna was used to these occasional fiery exchanges between Max and Harry, both of whom could display flashes of temper. She was good at choosing when to intervene to smooth ruffled feathers but she was glad that had not been necessary on this occasion. Now she could look forward to seeing Harry again the following week, and, she hoped, Arthur too. It would be a happy family gathering despite the political events putting everyone on edge.

Reichenberg, Friday 30 September 1938

The small lorry reversed slowly out of the yard and turned left along the cobbles, threading its way carefully through the narrow medieval streets, which Harry had come to know and love. The back of the lorry was uncomfortable. The presence of Otto Heller reduced the space even further; the two men obeyed the injunction to remain silent as they tried to find some comfort in the cramped space. Harry could feel Otto's shallow breathing and the odour of an expensive *eau de cologne* close to his face. Despite the dark he could just make out a taut grimace on Otto's face; he imagined he must look much the same. Aware of his heightened senses, he listened for every sound, felt every bump on the uneven road, smelt the diesel fumes trapped between the walls of the high buildings. The drumming he had heard earlier from his office was more insistent and menacing now. Despite the tarpaulin which both men had pulled down tightly, their hideout was occasionally illuminated by flickering lights from the burning torches being assembled for the victory march. The noise of the excited crowd was punctuated by shouts of "*Sieg Heil!*" and once again the ominous "*Juda verrecke!*" Harry's mind wandered to the exchange with his father only five days previously. He hoped his parents were safe and not cowering in the back of a vehicle speeding away from the home in which they had lived for nearly thirty years. And what of Arthur? Where was he? Safe, perhaps with his friends in Moravia, away from the turmoil of the Sudetenland.

Much had changed since the previous Monday night when he had returned from Trautenau. Harry followed events obsessively on the wireless and in the local newspapers. He knew that Neville Chamberlain, the British Prime Minister, had travelled to and fro from London to Bad Godesberg to negotiate with Hitler, ostensibly to preserve peace in Europe. There had been partial mobilisations in France and Britain, the Czech Army remained mobilised and ready to defend the independence of the young democracy. President Roosevelt had pleaded for peace as Europe stood on the brink of war. Then had come Benito Mussolini's last-minute *coup de théâtre*, the invitation for Chamberlain and the joint guarantor of Czechoslovak security, French Prime Minister, Edouard Daladier, to come to Munich to meet with the Führer and himself in one last desperate attempt to salvage peace. Harry had read reports of how Chamberlain had been greeted rapturously by the crowds in the streets of Munich and later in London when he had declared *"peace in our time"*. All was now clear. Britain and France would not stand by their international obligations and had capitulated on behalf of Czechoslovakia, to whose aid they would now not come. Deserted and abandoned by its friends, it lay defenceless. The Munich Agreement, signed earlier that day, had in effect negotiated Czechoslovakia out of existence. This much Harry understood.

In Reichenberg and throughout the Sudetenland preparations were in full swing to greet the liberators from the all-powerful Reich. The worst had come to pass and Dr Lewy was now fleeing for his life.

Gradually the lorry picked up speed. Alois and his cargo were now out on the open road heading east to where the line of demarcation would run between the territory soon to be incorporated into the enlarged Reich and what would remain of Czechoslovakia, beyond Nazi reach at least for the time being. Suddenly the lorry appeared to be turning right on to a rougher track before coming to a halt. A new frisson of fear gripped Harry. Where were they? What was happening now?

Then Alois was standing at the back of the lorry, tugging the tarpaulin away. The faintest light of the day was draining from the sky to the west as the sun set behind the Giant Mountains, Harry's *Heimat*, his *Riesengebirge*, for the Czechs, their *Krkonoše*.

"You can come out now", Alois said, "it's safe here, there are Czech patrols on the road and a checkpoint a few kilometres ahead. You don't need to hide any more, just sit on the bench behind the cab for the rest of the journey and say as little as possible."

"Where are we going?" Harry asked, although the answer did not matter so much any more as long as it was away from the forfeited areas.

"Dvůr Králové," Alois replied. "A reception centre or something similar has been set up there. You are not the only gentlemen on an errand like this tonight."

Harry felt re-assured that Alois, like his older brother equally at home in Czech or German, was the perfect person to be conveying them to safety along these country roads.

Alois reached into a bag and passed a bottle of beer and a wrapped sandwich to his passengers. Harry immediately recognised the smell of liver paste, not his favourite, but he felt grateful nonetheless. It had been many hours since he had had anything to eat. He was cold and hungry.

Dvůr Králové / Kōniginhof, Czechoslovakia, Saturday 1 October 1938

Midnight had passed when they finally reached their destination. The potholes on the road had been a minor inconvenience but the frequent Czech army patrols and then an unexpected Sudeten German *Freikorps* checkpoint had slowed their progress. It appeared that some agreement locally had been reached about how the Czechs would begin to pull back and the Germans move into position. Neither passengers nor driver knew for sure what dangers lay ahead but out on the open road pragmatic common sense had prevailed, both sides anxious to avoid a flare-up which could turn fatal.

Harry and Otto had exchanged only a few words. Neither had a plan. Neither knew what to do other than get away from the invading German forces and their jubilant local allies. A light drizzle had soaked them by the time the lorry drew to a halt at the reception tent in the centre of Dvůr Králové. The historic market square was in darkness apart from two storm lanterns which provided enough light for the official behind his desk to go through some perfunctory questions, make a few notes in a ledger and issue the new arrivals with a sheet of instructions in Czech and German, a slip of paper with an address and an envelope.

The *Penzion Hotelu Central* was a few steps away across the square. Low-key and in need of a lick of paint, it offered the prospect of shelter and a bed for the night. A dim light suggested that it had not yet shut. In his German accented Czech Harry explained that he and his friend had just arrived and were looking for a room. They were sorry for the late hour but there had been some delays on the way. The concierge smiled, took the envelopes which, it turned out, contained just the correct number of crowns to pay for the accommodation and ushered the two men along a narrow corridor which smelled of boiled cabbage.

"Here you are, room number four. Sleep well, gentlemen."

Two narrow beds filled the space. A thin curtain over the window, through which a yellowish light penetrated from the gas lamp in the street below, added a flicker of comfort. The carpet was stained and worn. A wash basin stood next to the door on which two pegs allowed for coats and hats.

"Welcome to the Ritz," murmured Harry.

Moments later he was deeply asleep and not even Otto's steady snoring nor the hotel's army of bed bugs could wake him.

As dawn broke and Harry emerged from a restless night, Otto Heller was already busy preparing to depart.

"I am moving on, Prague most likely, possibly Brno, I have a cousin there," he said, "as far away from here and the Germans as possible."

Harry was taken aback. He had not had time to think of his next step but his companion clearly had decided on a plan. Feeling uncertain and indecisive, he replied:

"I will sit it out here for a few days. I need to find out where my parents are and what is going on at home."

Otto picked up his case, shook Harry by the hand, wished him good fortune and expressed the hope they might meet again in happier times. He walked out of the room, leaving the door ajar.

Dvůr Králové, Tuesday 4 October 1938

On the fourth successive morning since his impromptu late-night arrival, Harry found himself standing under the arcades which surround the grand medieval square in the centre of Dvůr Králové. He awaited nervously the arrival of the buses he had been assured were on their way from Trautenau and due at around ten o'clock. Pulling the brim of his hat further down into his face he lit a cigarette, a substitute for the breakfast which he had foregone to save a few crowns. As had now become his daily routine, he positioned himself with a perfect view of the reception tent next to the historic fountain in the middle of the square. In better times, he would have admired the fine houses ringing the square above the arcades; he would have sipped a Viennese coffee, while enjoying a pastry or two and the customary cigarette as he read the day's news in one or more papers hanging on their wooden battens next to the coffee house door. These were not better times. His purpose was limited to hoping that his parents would be on one of the buses from Trautenau. It was only a few kilometres to the border between the Reich and the rump of Czechoslovakia. German soldiers had been seen at the station on the edge of town. Even a short journey could be perilous. Harry had no way of knowing whether the rumours of mass arrests by the Gestapo and stories of outrages by local Nazis against the remaining Jewish population were exaggerated. Would his parents' British passports be respected? Would they finally arrive this morning and reach relative safety?

The first bus drove into the square a quarter of an hour late and decanted its mainly elderly passengers who then formed a line, clutching suitcases which seemed too heavy for them to carry. Czech officials and volunteers wearing patriotic armbands in the blue, red and white national colours offered hot drinks and guided the newcomers to the makeshift registration desks in the tent. The atmosphere was subdued. Friends and family members who had assembled in expectation were held back by Czech gendarmes behind a cordon until registration was complete. There were embraces, a few quiet words were exchanged and the crowd dispersed. Harry's parents were not amongst the passengers. He turned to replenish his supply of cheap cigarettes from a stall on the corner, when a second bus appeared, smoky diesel fumes emanating from the exhaust.

"Thank God we're here," his father said as he and Minna emerged from the tent where they had given their personal details in exchange for a stamp in their passports.

They embraced tightly. Tears flowed gently over his mother's normally impassive face. They both looked fatigued, defeated and diminished, almost too tired to speak as if after a long ordeal, although in distance the journey itself had been very short. They each were carrying two suitcases and were wearing heavy overcoats despite the mild autumn morning. Harry led them across the square towards a coffee house in a side street.

"Let's have a bite to eat and something to drink," he said, "and then I can show you where we are staying." His father almost smiled.

•••

"I've managed to find us a couple of rooms," Harry told his parents as they sat in a quiet corner of the coffee house, "nothing much but it's clean and there's a little kitchen attached. I'm afraid the bathroom is down the corridor but it's better than nothing."

"Couldn't you find us a hotel?" his mother asked, "after all we won't be staying long, I hope."

Harry was irritated but made the necessary effort to conceal his feelings. Although they did not know what lay ahead of them, surely it was obvious to his mother this was not the usual kind of excursion or pleasure trip which periodically punctuated their placid lives in Trautenau.

"There was nothing available which I could afford," he explained, "the town's overwhelmed. There are hundreds of people here, everyone's looking for accommodation. People are frightened, desperate, refugees, outcasts in our own country."

Harry looked at his parents. They suddenly appeared to him rather shabby and bewildered. His father, normally meticulous about his appearance, was unshaven. His mother's expression betrayed sadness and confusion. They had not reacted to his description of them as refugees, as if assenting without question to their new and unwelcome status. They had all left a home where they were no longer welcome. Where they might come to rest was a question which he barely dared to ask and to which at that moment he knew he could find no answer.

He had spent hours walking the streets of the little town from one possible place to another in search of something suitable. Some rooms were dirty, others in back yards where rats scurried, others at prices suddenly inflated to take advantage of the unexpected boom in demand. His first searches had been fruitless. Reluctantly he returned to the *Penzion* for a second night, hoping the following day would be more successful. In the end he discovered the tiny apartment, big enough for his parents to have a room looking out across the red tiled roofs of the town. A small additional windowless broom-cupboard of a space with a single bed would be adequate for himself. The kitchen had running cold water, a small gas stove and a table with four chairs. An array of pots and pans, and a mixed selection of cutlery and crockery, much of it chipped, littered the few cupboards. The apartment was not as cheap as its quality would have merited but it was affordable; it would have to do.

"Let's go there now; you can at least leave your cases and have a rest." He picked up the two bigger cases. How heavy they are, he said quietly to himself, what have they packed?

His parents passively followed him tamely out of the door and across the square, a melancholy little procession.

Czechoslovakia at the time of the Munich Agreement. The Sudetenland, ceded to Germany, is shown by the shaded areas.

2.
LIMBO

Dvůr Králové, *Yom Kippur* evening, Tuesday 4 October 1938

The world as they knew it had been upended.

In the few days since Harry had joined his parents at the family home for their New Year celebrations everything had changed. He struggled to make sense of the world they now inhabited.

The *Yom Kippur* service began. Harry sat huddled close to his father on the narrow pew, sharing the prayer book which a stranger had pressed into his hand as he entered the synagogue. Glancing up towards the women's gallery he could see his mother sitting on the back row. She looked tired, gaunt, unhappy. His father seemed lost, enveloped in the stranger's prayer shawl. Harry scoured the unfamiliar faces in the congregation. Here and there he thought he recognised a fellow outsider, faces he knew vaguely from home, wan, disorientated and anxious.

He knew well the story of the *Kol Nidrei* service which ushers in *Yom Kippur*, the Day of Atonement, the solemn, sombre plea for forgiveness for transgressions committed throughout history, in times of menace and persecution. The Fast, the centrepiece of this ancient ritual, was now beginning and would last throughout the night and the following day until the final blast of the *Shofar*. Harry tried to immerse himself in the service, but his mind was on other things. He felt bitterness and anger. What exactly was he supposed to be repenting on this holiest of evenings? What precisely were his transgressions? What was he asking forgiveness for? From whom? He kept his thoughts to himself, partly out of deference to his father beside him and partly to keep under control the deep sense of anger rising within him. Was the visibly weary Max Lewy pondering similar questions? Was his faith stronger, more deeply engrained than that of his son? Did his parents draw greater sustenance than he could from the steadfastness of the familiar liturgy?

Harry recited silently not the words of the *Yom Yippur* prayers but of the Passover *Seder*, "*Mah nishtanah, ha-laylah ha-zeh, mi-kol ha-leylot? Why is this night different from all other nights?*"

A smile crossed his lips. "That's not right, is it?" he said under his breath. "I'm mixing things up." Despite the grimness of the situation Harry was fleetingly amused by his ironic irreverence and inappropriate frivolity. He could not let the thoughts go. They welled up inside him from a recess in his mind which he had not known existed. All this because I'm a Jew, it's that simple. *Yom Kippur, Pesach*, it doesn't really matter, does it? This is my fate, our fate, the fate of Jews throughout our history. This is what happens to us.

Harry could not at that moment have defined precisely what the "this" was, but he was suddenly aware of a consciousness, a feeling connecting him to a long history of persecution and displacement to which he had never previously devoted attention. The clarity with which he now understood his situation shocked him.

Of course, he knew why this *Kol Nidrei* evening on 4 October 1938 in a strange synagogue in a strange town was different from anything he had ever experienced. And of course, he knew this was not the celebration of the Passover deliverance, that there was no Moses beckoning the Israelites towards the Promised Land on this occasion. Yes, he had, in a way, packed his belongings and fled, as recounted in the *Haggadah* he had owned since childhood, but where was the Red Sea parting miraculously to deliver him and his parents to safety on the other side? If Passover celebrated liberation and hope, the promise of a Land of Milk and Honey, then this *Yom Kippur*, amidst fear and anxiety, removed from the comforting surroundings of home, seemed to Harry to foretell only pain and disaster.

His mind was racing. As the service proceeded in the background, he recalled his first conscious encounter with the imagery of the age-old hatred of Jews. Just turned 20 at the time, he had been exploring the *bouquinistes* along the Seine on a warm autumn afternoon during his stay in Paris when he had casually picked up a copy of Edouard Drumont's *La Parole Libre* and been confronted with the grotesque caricature of *Le Juif Errant*, the Wandering Jew. The image had nothing to do with him, he told himself. Drumont and his *Ligue antisemitique de France*, was the past; Captain Alfred Dreyfus, once unjustly accused of betraying military secrets to Germany had been found innocent and rehabilitated after a long campaign which had bitterly divided the country. He could see no connection between the virulent anti-Jewish sentiment which had ravaged France then and his own cheerful freewheeling student existence in the City of Light.

Later, he had chosen to ignore occasional crude anti-Semitic remarks overheard in Viennese coffee houses and university lecture halls, dismissing them as no more than the mouthing of slogans by the ignorant and uneducated. In any event they had not been directed at him personally. He knew all about the popular appeal of *Bürgermeister* Karl Lueger's notorious anti-Jewish rhetoric but that too dated back to before the Great War.

Neither he nor his parents, as far as he knew, had ever been a direct target for anti-Semitic insults or attacks. Like all Jews, they knew about the Hilsner Affair and of the role T.G. Masaryk, later President Masaryk, had played in defending the Jewish vagrant, Leopold Hilsner, accused of murdering a young Christian girl to use her blood in a ritual sacrifice. That too was far in the past and Masaryk had died the previous year. The Lewys were a normal respectable family at home and at ease in a modern democratic republic. They fitted well into the comfortable middle-class society of the town until events across the border had begun to make an impact.

"What is normal?" he mused under his breath, oblivious to the congregation around him. "Am I also to become a Wandering Jew? Are we all? Is that the future?"

He had not recognised himself or his family in the hateful images he knew were being widely peddled in Germany and Austria, not just in extremist circles on the margins of society but by the Nazi state itself.

He tried again to concentrate on the service.

•••

It was already dark when the service ended. The Fast had begun. There was none of the usual conversation as they trudged back to their temporary home, taking in the strange surroundings of a

Czech town going about its normal business despite the proximity of the German forces and the imminence of invasion. They noticed occasional small convoys of Czech army units moving slowly through the narrow streets and snatches of German from passersby, similarly displaced and seeking refuge.

Assembled at the table in the small kitchen making do as a living room, they looked at each other, forlorn. The table was bare on this day of fasting apart from a small family photograph of parents and sons which Minna had quietly placed in the middle, a remembrance of unity in happier times.

Where has Arthur got to? Harry wondered silently for them all, was he safe, well away from the border areas? How could they contact him? Did he know that they were no longer in Trautenau?

Harry spoke first, aware that he might be usurping his father's role in taking the lead in family matters.

"So, what next?" His father shrugged in response. "We ought to make a plan," Harry continued, "we can't just sit here and wait for events."

"What do you suggest?" his father asked. "Should we not just see how things develop?" He paused. "I could contact the British Embassy in Prague and talk to my friend, Captain Taylor. I'm sure he will be able to help."

"Help how?" Harry replied. "Are you thinking of going somewhere? South Africa? Britain? The same Britain which has just betrayed us, sold us down the river to Hitler, for Mr Chamberlain's little scrap of paper?"

Harry was surprised at his own vehemence but carried on regardless, "and will your Captain Taylor suddenly give me a British passport? Or Arthur, who doesn't even speak a word of English? In any case I've heard that Captain Taylor is in Vienna these days."

Max did not rise to the challenge.

"First of all there is our house and our property. It's British property. The Germans can't just help themselves. It's ours by right. The British authorities have to make that clear to everyone."

He continued in a strictly practical vein, "we also need to go to the bank and get some money. We have to have something to live on."

"British property?", Harry retorted, "do you really think the fine gentlemen from the Gestapo will show respect for Reichstrasse 25 because it is British property? For them it is, or more precisely, was Jewish property, plain and simple and that suits them just fine."

Max ignored the comment.

"And then we can see if we can find something more suitable than this," he said, "even if we are only here for a few days, more comfortable lodgings would be a good idea."

"Let's not argue, "Harry said, placing his hand on his father's arm, "everything has happened so quickly. It's hard to take it all in. We're all a bit out of sorts."

Open in front of them on the table lay Max's British passport. At the bottom of the page was a freshly stamped addition indicating that the bearer had arrived in Dvůr Králové earlier that day, 4 October 1938. It was only a few hours since he had left Trautenau but it already seemed half a lifetime ago.

"Did they stamp yours as well when you registered?" Max asked.

"No," he replied, "the Czechs don't stamp Czech passports inside Czechoslovakia."

He had not wanted to sound tetchy but was aware of the bitterness underlying his response.

He did not have the protection of a British passport. He could not claim to be a foreigner.

More than the Fast, the absence of tobacco was taking its toll on his nerves. For the second time in recent days he realised how much he had come to depend on his cigarettes. At least it's not alcohol, he thought.

"I'll just get some fresh air. I won't be long," he said, rising from the table and slipping on his coat. Max recognised his son's strategy for avoiding conflict and was grateful for it. It was one he himself deployed many times, when he and Minna had not seen eye to eye on some usually trivial domestic matter.

"Don't forget your hat," his mother reminded him. Harry could not resist a boyish grin. Did a man of nearly thirty really need his mother to tell him what to wear? Some things never change, he mused.

He opened the door, proceeded down the corridor and stairs and into the quiet streets. His outward appearance, he assumed, suggested a comfortably off, well-dressed youngish gentleman calmly enjoying a walk in the cool evening air. Alternatively, he wondered, was it all too apparent to any onlooker that here was yet another disoriented stranger, down on his luck, with nowhere to go? Nothing betrayed his inner disarray. After the best part of an hour of aimlessly walking, glancing into shop windows and battling with the temptation to resort to a cigarette despite the Fast, he returned. His parents had already gone to bed. He slipped into his broom cupboard bedroom, lay down and closed his eyes.

•••

Dvůr Králové, Wednesday 9 November 1938 – early morning

Full of expectation Max boarded the morning bus to Prague outside the post office in the centre of Dvůr Králové.

Undertaking the journey to Prague on this grey November day, he was hopeful he might finally resolve an issue which had rankled with him for many years but was now urgent. A passionately loyal subject of the British Empire, he had always firmly believed that, in time of need, His Britannic Majesty would provide not just for himself and Minna but also for his two sons. He had assembled a formidable list of documents going back to the service he had rendered the Empire in South Africa in time of war nearly 40 years previously. He had marshalled his proud arguments, rehearsing them to himself more than once during the long journey.

An uneasy calm had been re-established in the aftermath of German occupation of its newly acquired territory. The Czech authorities, clearly on edge, suspected German infiltrators and saboteurs everywhere. Progress was slow on account of the numerous checkpoints on the road towards Prague. Just outside Hradec Králové the bus encountered a road-block manned by a platoon of heavily armed soldiers.

"Everyone off!" commanded a young steel-helmeted Czech soldier armed with a sub-machine gun, as he stepped on to the bus. "Line up! Get your documents ready for inspection!"

Max stepped down clutching his leather briefcase containing all his valuable papers. Looking round at his fellow passengers, he could pick out those who, like him, had known better times and whose anxious faces bore the marks of recent upheaval. Was that as obvious to the soldiers? Taking his place in the queue, he could overhear that only few of the passengers were native Czech speakers. The soldiers made no concessions and addressed the travellers abruptly in Czech, issuing instructions and gesticulating where appropriate to add emphasis. Soon it was Max's turn.

"I am a British citizen," he explained as confidently as the situation permitted. "I am travelling to Prague on business," Max continued in impeccable but accented English, presenting his distinctive blue passport with pride whilst straining to conceal any trace of a German accent.

The soldiers evidently spoke no English but a glance at the passport sufficed. A flick of a finger indicated that Max could resume his seat. When the bus finally departed several seats were now empty. Max observed a couple of former passengers who had aroused the suspicions of the anxious soldiers, being led away under guard. He felt unnerved. Not for the first time in his life he was grateful for his British passport.

Finally he arrived in Prague in good time to register at his hotel and to attend punctually for the appointment he had made for two o'clock in the afternoon.

•••

He was glad he knew the way to the Consulate and did not have to rely on his imperfect Czech to ask for directions. He threaded his way through the maze of narrow winding streets from his hotel in the Old Town down towards the river and crossing Charles Bridge, he noted, as he always did, the Hebrew inscription on a statue of the crucifixion on the famous bridge. He began the ascent up the ancient street towards the Castle. Reaching the consulate building he was taken aback by the large noisy crowd at the gates, shouting, demanding, pleading. He needed both his substantial frame and his passport to force his way through and gain admission. The guard at the entrance eyed him with suspicion, differently from the friendly smile which usually greeted him on his previous visits.

"British, are you?" he asked with menace in his voice. Max showed his passport but remained silent.

"You may proceed, Mr Lewy," the guard consented coldly after a lengthy pause and with evident lack of enthusiasm, ushering him through the hostile comments from those whose further progress had been terminated. This was not the kind of welcome he had once enjoyed. Over the years he had visited many times, to renew documents, to sign the book of condolences when King George V had died and to receive in person from the ambassador a letter of thanks for his endeavours on behalf of the Earl Haig Fund.

•••

Prague, 9 November 1938 – early afternoon
"I am very sorry indeed, sir, but I do not see there is much more His Majesty's Government can do to assist at present. The rules are quite clear."

"I am a loyal British citizen," Max replied, "surely that counts for something in these difficult times?"

"Indeed it does," replied the official, "indeed it does. You and Mrs Lewy have every right to travel to the United Kingdom whenever you wish."

"And my sons? I am worried about my sons. What's going to happen to them? Life is becoming impossible here. Our home is now in Hitler's Reich. The Czechs hate us and say we're Germans. The Germans know we're Jews. They're hell-bent on driving us out. What are we supposed to do? Where are we to go?"

"As I have already explained, "the official replied, labouring his studied patience, "His Majesty will consider you and your wife welcome whenever you choose to visit."

"But my sons, Harry, Arthur, what about them?"

"Ah, that is an entirely different matter. As you well know, they are citizens of Czechoslovakia or Czecho-Slovakia, as we now call this country. Much as I would like to assist you, Mr Lewy, I cannot simply issue British passports to anyone who presents himself at His Majesty's Embassy or Consulate claiming to be displaced or in some sort of danger."

"Furthermore," he added after a brief pause, "as I have already explained to you, neither son was born in the United Kingdom nor one of its dominions or colonies. As far as His Majesty's Government is concerned, it is very straightforward. They are foreigners; the foreign born sons of a naturalised British subject. They have no entitlement to a British passport and no automatic right to enter the United Kingdom."

"Even if they are in danger?"

"Danger?" repeated the official, raising an eyebrow to express his evident scepticism, "aren't we perhaps exaggerating just a little?"

Max suppressed his frustration. There was no point provoking the vice consul into further condescension. He looked despairingly around the office, his eyes coming to rest on a portrait of the young king. He gazed at it, as if asking him directly and personally for help. He turned back to the official.

"So what do you suggest?"

"Well, perhaps they could apply to visit for an extended stay as tourists until things calm down a bit more and it is safer to return. You know the kind of thing, sight-seeing, a bit of shopping for luxury items one cannot find in Prague." The vice consul paused before returning to his theme.

"Now, wouldn't that be a good idea? I am sure they are not short of a pound or two. Shouldn't be too difficult!" He paused again, aware of Max's impassive face.

"Alternatively, perhaps another country might be prepared to grant entry, even citizenship. I am told that Uruguay is open to such arrangements, in exchange for an appropriate fee. I assume that would not be a problem for a prosperous gentleman like yourself, Mr Lewy."

•••

Max only just contained his exasperation. He well understood the implications in the vice consul's remarks. Nothing in the past had caused him to doubt his prestigious status as a British subject. A bitter moment of doubt now crossed his mind.

Is this what … *allow the bearer to pass freely without let or hindrance and to afford him every assistance and protection* – actually amounts to? he asked himself, as he made his way down the stairs and out into the street, where noisy crowds were still gathered.

•••

Deflated and troubled, he picked his way carefully along Thunovská, down through the Lesser Town towards the river. His anticipation of assistance from sympathetic officials had been seriously misguided. In its place he had encountered the blank face of unfeeling bureaucracy which he had always associated with the Austro-Hungarian but not his beloved British Empire. Superficially courteous and correct in his manner, the official had been utterly intransigent. There would be no British passports for the offspring of this British subject, originally German but naturalised in a colony over thirty years previously in recognition of service rendered to the Empire. That was the end of the matter. Max fought back a powerful feeling of disillusion. The great national betrayal at Munich now had its personal counterpart in Prague. Perhaps Harry had been more realistic all along about the prospects for success of his expedition to the capital. He would break the unwelcome news to Minna, waiting in Dvůr Králové. He anticipated she would not take it well.

Prague, 9 November 1938 – early evening
Darkness was falling as he reached *U Tři Bubnu* hotel not far from the Old Town Square. He slowly made his way up to his room on the second floor, took the heavy brass key from the pocket of his overcoat, unlocked the door and surveyed the scene. It was a modest hotel to be sure but an improvement nonetheless on their current accommodation.

Earlier in the day he had been in a hurry. "Not the Savoy," he had muttered to himself, "but it'll do. I had better make the right impression. I am Max Lewy, Flax Merchant and I am here as a British Subject on official business" he rehearsed to himself.

Standing in front of the mirror on the dresser he continued his monologue as he extracted the precious briefcase from the suitcase lying on the bed.

"A change of shirt would be in order and I'm going nowhere without my leather briefcase," before adding softly, "I'm not fooling anyone," a sadness in his subdued voice.

He would go through with his plan to convince the officials at the Consulate of the justice of his case. Of course, they would be pleased to assist him.

Gone was the time when Max, always careful about money, had indulged himself in the fleeting luxury of the Palace Hotel on his occasional business trips to Prague.

Now, reviewing his failure, Max gazed out of his hotel bedroom window. In the gathering gloom he could just make out the renaissance clock on the tower of the old Jewish Town Hall. On his first visit to Prague decades previously he had felt intrigued and excited by the bustle and vitality of the city, a contrast after years of adventures in South Africa. How well he remembered continuing his journey to Trautenau to meet his bride-to-be after a week in a smart hotel on elegant Pařižská on the edge of the former ghetto.

He had always felt at ease in the Czech capital. Now all was confusion.

Tired, hungry and unhappy at how the afternoon had turned out, Max could not deny to himself the thinly concealed hostility of the consular official beneath the veneer of diplomatic courtesy with which he had been greeted. He felt humiliated, betrayed and slowly fearful.

•••

He had picked up a copy of the *Prager Tagblatt*, his favourite newspaper and the voice of liberal, democratic opinion, as he had walked through the hotel lobby on arrival and then left it lying next to his suitcase. He glanced at the headline: '*Incident in Paris*'. He would get round to reading the paper later that evening. First, he wanted to freshen up, get some air and find a discreet little place for his evening meal. There were plenty of acceptable restaurants nearby where he could find something reasonably priced and which reflected his reduced circumstances.

He had looked forward to spoiling himself in celebration of his anticipated triumph at the Consulate. His spirits were low now. Taking his passport out of the briefcase he studied the new stamp dated that day, 9 November 1938, and the hand-written annotation stating the passport was valid until 27 October 1939. At least he had accomplished something, he convinced himself, before surrendering to the truth that his mission to obtain protection for his two sons had come to nothing. He could not escape that brutal reality as he speculated on what this might mean. He dismissed the painful train of thought that was beginning to take shape.

He knew Prague was full of people fleeing from the Reich, hoping to get as far away as their meagre resources would permit. Would the Lewy family be forced to join them, Max worried. Now that the Germans had breached the country's natural defences, was Prague actually safe? Beneš had left the country. Repressive anti-Jewish laws had been swiftly enacted. Was it only a matter of time until Hitler's next move? The Czechs did not welcome the latest influx of indigents. The newspaper headlines made that clear. Was the afternoon's rebuff a foretaste of future disappointment and difficulty?

A hearty meal and a glass of dark Smichov beer in a dimly lit cellar restaurant serving 'good-value traditional Bohemian specialities' failed to console him. He felt sick at heart, unsettled, as he weighed up the implications of his futile journey.

Dvůr Králové, Thursday 10 November 1938
"Thank God you're back," Minna exclaimed, embracing Max with an unaccustomed public display of emotion as he stepped down from the bus. "It's terrible, terrible," she continued, "what are we going to do?"

Max was taken aback. He had not expected his wife and son to be waiting for him at the bus stop. After all, it was only a few paces to their rooms.

Minna sounded distraught. Harry said nothing but looked drawn. Max was perplexed at the apparent change which had taken place within the short time he had been away.

"So you haven't heard?" Minna persisted.

"Heard what?"

"It's just too awful." Tears filled her eyes. Harry looked away. Evidently his father had not the slightest idea of what had transpired since he had set off for Prague the previous morning.

"Let's get home first and then we'll tell you everything," he suggested, guiding his father firmly by the arm in the general direction of their lodgings.

Prague and Dvůr Králové, 10 November 1938

Max had spent the morning in Prague strolling aimlessly along the principal shopping streets, killing time before catching the bus home and trying to avoid brooding on the events of the previous afternoon which had led to a sleepless night. He wanted to look for a small gift he might bring for Minna for her birthday which he had missed because of his appointment at the Consulate. He had immersed himself in a couple of bookshops; nothing had caught his eye but in the end he had found a collection of recently translated stories by Somerset Maugham and a pretty bracelet at a street stall. They would have to suffice.

Shortly after midday he had boarded the bus. Once again there had been delays with frequent checkpoints on the roads the further north they went towards the border regions. Czech soldiers searched each vehicle and scrutinised each passenger's documents. A stout gentleman in his sixties was not really the stuff of spies or saboteurs, Max decided, as a corporal rummaged perfunctorily through his case.

He had not looked at the newspaper he had picked up the afternoon before, resolving instead to keep it as reading material for the bus journey north.

A shooting in Paris, reported the newspaper, but without much by way of further detail, other than that a junior German diplomat had been attacked and was in a serious condition in hospital. There was something about the alleged assailant, apparently a Jew, now in the custody of the Paris police. Max, preoccupied with his own worries, had not given the report further thought. On the bus neither he nor his fellow passengers, mainly Czechs, were inclined to start a conversation. Settled into a seat to the rear he dozed off for a good part of the journey. Progress was slow; he arrived almost two hours late which perhaps explained his wife's agitation. Her tendency to worry for no good reason, to make a fuss about nothing, was not a novelty.

He walked alongside Harry and Minna, unable to make sense of their mood. The day was gone by the time they climbed the stairs to their make-shift home.

"So," said Max, settling himself in command of the small kitchen table, "what's happened, what's this all about?"

As calmly as possible, Harry began. From time to time, his mother added a comment which sounded more like a lamentation.

TRAUTENAU SYNAGOGUE, built 1882, destroyed 9 November 1938. Today a ruin.

Trautenau, Grossdeutsches Reich, 9-10 November 1938

The mixture of thugs and apparently respectable citizens who made up the local SA storm-troopers in Trautenau, in their brown shirts and black boots, had not been slow to get to work. Everything had changed in the time it had taken Max to travel to and from Prague. Late on Wednesday evening gangs of men and youths had begun to gather in the main town square, shouting and chanting. Someone made an inflammatory speech to the crowd: the Jews would pay for their crimes. Without warning, a procession had formed and marched out of the square to the nearby Rinnelstrasse. Stones were thrown, seemingly at random, and the sound of breaking glass could be heard. Then the crowd, by now a mob, came to a standstill outside the town's synagogue. Men appeared with flaming torches which they hurled against the wooden doors of the building. Another torch and then more were thrown through a broken window. The mob had grown in number to include women and children, laughing, singing and dancing wildly. To one side the town's fire brigade stood inactive, watching the spectacle. By shortly after midnight the building was well alight. The crowd cheered jubilantly.

As dawn broke, all that remained were smoking ruins and a pungent smell in the air. Outside the town's small number of Jewish-owned businesses the signs of the overnight rampage were everywhere to be seen. The plate-glass shop window and front of the S.A.Katz shop on Schlesischestrasse had been reduced to rubble, the wall daubed with obscenities.

With the synagogue ablaze, the mob had followed its night-time destruction with a hunt for human victims. Lists had been prepared. A column of Jewish men, some very elderly, some still no more than boys, had been assembled on the central square, under a hail of abuse from onlookers. One or two had clearly been beaten. Later, in the middle of the morning, lorries arrived to take them away. Some private houses had been attacked but a cordon of SA men now ensured that opportunist looting was kept to a minimum. Announcements over loudspeakers praised the population for its restraint in the face of monstrous Jewish provocation but, the announcer warned, the wrath of the people could not be ignored. What had taken place should not be misunderstood. Further Jewish misdeeds and outrages would not go unpunished. Jews would pay a high price for their criminal insolence.

Dvůr Králové, 10 November 1938
From morning onwards a trickle of women and children arrived in Dvůr Králové. Harry, looking for flowers for his mother's birthday, had seen the first frightened group stagger from the bus. He recognised

two former neighbours from Reichstrasse. Their eyewitness accounts were confirmed later in the day as reports began to appear in the papers and on the small secondhand wireless he had acquired, thanks to the generosity, or more precisely the business acumen, of the concierge of the building where they now lodged. Harry felt that he had struck a good bargain, paying only a few crowns each week for the loan of the rickety apparatus which now assumed the status of a luxury yet essential item in the sparse rooms.

Max listened, stunned.

"A pogrom," he said finally, before sinking into a profound silence, "a pogrom, here in the heart of Europe. We've seen it all before. Kishinev again, after all"

Max listened, stunned.

TRAUTENAU: The Ringplatz renamed Adolf-Hitler-Platz, 1940

Dvůr Králové, Friday, 11 November 1938

By the next morning the scale of events had become much clearer. They had listened to the triumphant wireless reports from across the border. An exultant newsreader announced that in Cologne, Hamburg, Berlin and many other cities, synagogues, shops and private houses had gone up in flames. The Jews well deserved the punishment meted out to them, to their places of worship and their property. It extended across the Reich, from centres of major historic Jewish communities to small towns and rural and isolated locations, from Germany to Austria to the newly incorporated Sudetenland. The Jews, the exultant newsreader proclaimed, had brought upon themselves the just retribution and righteous anger of the German nation.

What had occurred in Trautenau was not an isolated incident caused by a few local hotheads and an excess of alcohol. Reichenberg, Brüx, Troppau, the heart of the Sudetenland, had all fallen victim to an organized premeditated wave of nationwide assaults. Later came reports of whole-scale arrests of Jewish men; concentration camps in Dachau, Buchenwald and Sachsenhausen were receiving many thousands of prisoners. Later still they were to learn of suicides and deaths and the crippling fine imposed on the Jews for their alleged crimes.

The German authorities stated that the outbreaks of disorder were spontaneous expressions of German anger and patriotism following the treacherous assassination of Ernst vom Rath in Paris by a renegade Jewish criminal. Vom Rath had died two days after the attack, on the very evening Max had been in Prague. German radio stations reported that the outraged German people could not be restrained from taking matters into its own hands before the forces of law and order could intervene to restore calm.

"Spontaneous! Like hell, spontaneous!". Max exploded. "How can they get away with it? What was the police doing, the fire brigade? The rest of the world must intervene and put a stop to this madness!"

"And if they come here, what will they do to us?" asked Minna despairingly. "Nowhere is safe for us. What are we to do?"

"Turn the damned radio off," said Harry, getting up to extinguish the immediate source of their pain.

•••

Harry decided not to accompany his father to the synagogue for the start of the Sabbath service that evening; neither had the family held its usual Friday night celebratory meal on Max's return to welcome the Sabbath. A perfunctory cold snack had sufficed, although the candles had been lit and Max had pronounced a brief blessing. The emerging news of the events of the two previous days hung over them, a black impenetrable and ominous cloud. Max reported on snatched exchanges of news at the synagogue. Any previous complacency some may have harboured that they would be spared the Nazi frenzy by dint of living in a foreign country, was now shattered. Apprehension and mounting panic prevailed.

Max and Minna had then retreated early to bed, leaving Harry alone with his bleak anxieties. In the morning he still felt troubled. A walk would help him to clear his head, where all was a tumult of confusion. He needed to think straight.

By the end of that gloomy November Saturday, the Lewy family had come to fateful decisions.

After the morning service Max once again joined some of his fellow worshippers on the steps of the building. The congregation had shrunk in numbers in the course of October, despite the growing influx from across the new border. Details, rumours and speculation were exchanged, giving grounds for deep pessimism. Worshippers spoke openly. There could be no future for them here in what remained of Czechoslovakia; their very existence was imperilled. Failing to act was as dangerous potentially as making the wrong move. Max, who tended to keep himself to himself, listened, absorbing the information but contributing nothing other than a brief description of the frantic crowd outside the British Embassy he had witnessed earlier in the week.

Anxiety was palpable.

"What is to become of us?" wailed an overwrought young man, tears running down his sallow face. "The Nazis want us Jews out. The Czechs don't want us either. We're caught."

He looked round despairingly for others to agree. "What are we supposed to do? Where are we supposed to go? We can't go on like this!"

"So, what do you suggest?" challenged a voice. The crowd fell silent. They all knew there was no easy answer to the question. There was no agreement, no obvious response to the young man nor to his challenger. Panic gripped the group.

"My father was taken away by the SA," said another man, his voice quivering with emotion.

"My brother too," added a young man who had previously said nothing, "they beat him up. He had cuts on his face. There was blood everywhere."

"We need to resist, to organise," interjected a third.

"How?" came a plaintive voice, "how do we do that?"

•••

Max drifted away and slowly made his way home, lost in thought as he sought a solution to a seemingly impossible problem. By the time he had reached the door to the lodgings, he had at least come to one conclusion. To do nothing and simply wait to see how things might turn out would put them all in even greater danger.

Minna, busying herself with the preparation of a frugal lunch and endless tidying up of their paltry possessions which did not require further tidying, was in her own fashion coming to a similar conclusion. What had begun as a temporary measure to avoid some local trouble could not become a permanent way of living one's life. Until a few weeks ago they had enjoyed the relative luxury of a spacious house, material prosperity and a respected place in society and the Jewish community. She was now struggling to come to terms with the possibility that the sudden disruption to an orderly, secure world was not just a momentary aberration but the shape of what might lie ahead.

After lunch, Harry took his leave, explaining he was meeting an acquaintance to discuss the situation they were facing. Minna was uncertain about how Max might react but no longer suppressed what was going through her mind. She took her husband by the hand and said gently, almost inaudibly, "Max, we need to talk. Come, sit down next to me."

Max recognized immediately that this was to be one of those rare but significant occasions which had punctuated their over thirty years of married life when Minna, usually happy for him to take the lead in family matters, would assert herself. They sat close to each other and for a while allowed a solemn silence to prevail. Then, turning to look him directly in the eye, Minna took both his hands.

"Max," she said quietly, "it's over here. We both know it. We can't stay here much longer, it's not safe for people like us. There's danger everywhere."

Max sighed but did not on this occasion interrupt. She continued: "Yes, we have British passports, and they may help but they aren't an absolute guarantee. You know that, too, don't you?"

"Yes, I know," he said.

"I read the newspapers, just like you, I talk to people. I know what is happening and I am frightened, for us and for the boys. And I had a letter the other day from Rachel Goldberg. You remember the Goldbergs, neighbours in Reichstrasse who moved to Frankfurt about seven or eight years ago? Well, Rachel says life has become impossible there and they are desperate to get out of Germany."

"So what are we to do?" asked Max, "have you thought about that?"

"Of course I have," she said, "what do you think I do, all day, every day?"

"No, I didn't mean that," Max replied. "I worry about what is happening all the time, but I don't know what we can do. I sometimes think it would be best to just sit this out and keep our heads down. This Nazi nightmare can't go on forever; things will change. Perhaps we should return home to Trautenau, keep out of sight and wait till everything returns to normal."

"No!" Minna's rejoinder was sharp, decisive. "I am neither deaf nor blind. And I am not a fool either! We are not going back."

He trusted Minna's judgement. It had been her powerfully strong personality which had sustained her throughout her painful childhood years following the death of her parents and the departure for America of her beloved brother, Sam. An orphan, alone in the world, it had been her decision to accept the offer from distant relatives in Trautenau to move to live with them and to abandon the final year of school at the Girls' *Gymnasium* in Memel, where she had shown so much promise.

Another long awkward silence ensued before Minna took up the theme once again, as if she was following a carefully prepared script.

"Czechoslovakia's finished. We don't even speak the language, we don't have Czechoslovak nationality. We don't belong here any more. Hitler will walk in whenever it suits him and they won't be able to do anything about it. And they don't want us anyway."

"Yes," Max agreed.

"Then there's Palestine," she continued, "but I don't think we are wanted there either. The Arabs certainly don't want any more of us. Palestine is for young people."

"What about your brother?" asked Max, "we could always ask him to help us."

"Times are hard; he always writes how much he is struggling, how he has two jobs just to make ends meet and how very different life in Paterson and New Jersey is from what he still calls 'home'. In any case, visas are hard to come by and it is so far away. America was maybe once a dream but not now, it's too far."

"South Africa, we could go back there."

"We, Max, we?" The derision in her voice made Max retreat as she continued, "to re-live the adventures of your bachelor days of forty years ago."

"No, of course not," he muttered, "I'm not really thinking straight."

"We will go to England," she declared emphatically. "You speak the language and I can manage a few phrases. We will be safe in England."

"Even after Munich?" he queried.

"Yes, even after Munich," she replied, getting up and flourishing the precious blue documents which lay on the sideboard, "we are British subjects. They told you in Prague that we would be welcome there." She paused. "Do you believe them?"

"Yes, I do. At least I think I believe them." Minna noticed the hesitation in his voice. Perhaps he was not quite so sure after all. "What about the boys?" Max continued.

"The boys are grown men, Max, young and resourceful. Harry will be thirty in February and Arthur is twenty-seven. They will have to make their own way and without delay. At least we have our passports."

And with that the matter was decided. It was Minna who had taken the fateful decision which would affect them all. She and Max would choose the time to talk to Harry about what they had in mind for themselves but first, he and Arthur needed to get to safety.

•••

PROSPERITY. Flax Merchant, Max Lewy, stands proudly outside the family home, Reichstrasse 25 – mid 1930s?

The continuing wrangle about their house and its contents with the Gestapo in Trautenau, conducted by proxies and by correspondence, was an indication that even what was theirs by right was not safeguarded.

A short letter had arrived from Trautenau that morning. Despite the tension on the new line demarcating the *Grossdeutsches Reich* and remaining Czechoslovakia, some postal services still managed to function. It was from Kurt, who had agreed, albeit reluctantly, to make representations to the new authorities there about Max and Minna's house.

Enclosed was an envelope bearing a swastika and the words *Geheime Staatspolizei, Dienststelle Trautenau*. Max fished out a single sheet and read aloud:

> Reference: Reichstrasse 25. This building and all adjacent land and outhouses, having been abandoned by the previous occupant, have been confiscated and are now the property of the German Reich. If the Jew, Lewy, cares to present himself in person to the local Gestapo within 30 days, the said Authority will be delighted to discuss with him his assertion that he is the lawful owner of the said property.
>
> Heil Hitler!

They glanced at each other. There would be no going back.

• • •

Harry applied himself to the task of analysing the situation. A multitude of ideas and insights flooded his mind where a feeling of deep unease and anxiety lurked, all leading inexorably to the same point. He too had reluctantly come to accept that his current existence was untenable in the longer term, that the length of that longer term was imponderable and very possibly much shorter than one might imagine. Hesitation itself could be as dangerous as a wrong step or an ill-judged decision.

Sitting discreetly in a corner of the coffee house, Harry pored over the morning's news, taking one newspaper after another from the rack and opening them on the table in front of him. The international press only rarely reached this far from the capital but the *Prager Tagblatt* still managed to get through. Reports of the pogrom across the Reich filled many columns but it was the banner headline which grabbed his attention.

"*Momentous times – we must face reality!*" He read on:

> "The Czechoslovakia we have known for twenty years no longer exists. Its territorial integrity has been destroyed. The first president of our fledgling country, T. G. Masaryk, was the incarnation of the highest humanistic values. He is no more. His successor, Edvard Beneš, resigned last month in the face of intolerable pressure from a mortal enemy, Germany. Mr Beneš has now left the country. The democracies we loved and admired so ardently have abandoned us. Our little country, once a beacon of liberal democracy, is no more. We are breaking apart, drifting towards the fascism of our neighbours. We are descending into an ugly, xenophobic authoritarianism. Our Second Republic bears no resemblance to its predecessor. And what is to be done with our and everybody else's Jews?

Harry took a deep breath and gulped down the remains of his coffee which had turned cold as he was reading.

"Yes, not so very far from the mark," he reflected, inhaling deeply and re-reading the final sentence. It cut to the quick: "*What is to be done with our and everybody else's Jews?*"

Understanding slowly crystallised. He was living in a very different country now, a foreigner in his own homeland. The newspaper summed up with brutal frankness the situation of the Lewys and thousands like them with deadly precision.

German and Austrian refugees from Nazism had found a short-lived haven in Czechoslovakia. The outsiders had not been welcomed by many Czechs. The government, following the capitulation at Munich, had adopted a harder, repressive line. There were stories that some who had escaped across the new border had been forced back into Germany to an uncertain fate. Anti-Semitism, always latent in the Czech lands and Slovakia, was rapidly becoming more evident.

Harry weighed up the limited enthusiasm for protecting German-speaking Jews like himself and his family. The lofty ideals of the First Republic had vanished like the Republic itself. Newly truncated Czecho-Slovakia could not or would not offer him the safety he had previously assumed. Danger, however ill-defined, now existed everywhere. Jews like him had become a problem. It was only a short step to being stripped of all rights, as was happening in Germany, and being made a pariah, fair game for anyone who wished to take advantage of their vulnerability. The idea of abandoning his home and all that he and his family had established, until recently inconceivable, had finally taken root for want of viable alternatives. Where, he asked himself as he gazed out of the coffee house window at the banal normality of life on the town square, where might he ever again feel secure, at home and at ease? Nowhere sprang to mind as he trudged back to their lodgings.

•••

Harry marvelled at his mother's genius. How did she construct a delicious chicken broth from so little? Saturday lunch that day was warming but ultimately insubstantial. His mother, never an extravagant cook, was even by her own standards, being unusually economical. Nonetheless the soup tasted good; it tasted of home.

Max presided. Harry loved and respected his father despite his penchant for occasional pomposity; this threatened to be one such occasion.

"I was born," Max started what to Harry sounded like the beginning of a familiar speech, " in what today is known as Lithuania. I grew up surrounded by Germans of the Prussian variety, Poles, Lithuanians, Russians and of course Jews. I spoke German and Yiddish, a smattering of Russian too."

SOUTH AFRICA – Max, the British citizen ca 1905

Harry doubted his father's autobiographical recitation was going to reveal some startling new information.

"As a young man, younger than you are today, Harry," Max continued, "I left my homeland on the Baltic to seek my fortune in Africa, in the Transvaal, in what is today part of the Union of South Africa. I lived there surrounded by the Dutch, that's to say the Boers, the British and the Hottentots. I didn't find gold and diamonds but I made a good life for myself there. I was accepted and became British."

Harry wanted to tell his father to get to the point but hesitated. Despite a mounting sense of urgency, now was not the moment for him to display impatience. They were all feeling strained. Max had clearly prepared what he was saying to them. Harry deferred once again. He felt his father was holding forth largely for his benefit.

"When I returned to Europe to marry your mother, I came to Trautenau in Austria-Hungary, later and until a few weeks ago, Czechoslovakia. We lived here for over thirty years. We prospered. I founded a family and a business as a flax merchant; we were happy, respected and respectable. We were surrounded by Germans and Czechs, Jews and Gentiles. We were at home. We had no enemies and got on with everyone. I expected to see out my days where I had lived and worked for half my life."

MARRIED: The happy couple 1907

"And now?" interjected Harry, impatient, despite himself.

"And now," said Max quietly, "and now, I see things differently. Now, as an old man of sixty-four, I see everything that I built up is being taken from me, from you, Harry, and from Arthur, from us all. We have no future here, only a past. I am condemned to be the eternal Wandering Jew. We all are. We cannot remain here in Dvůr Králové. We cannot return to Trautenau."

Max had come to the same realisation which Harry too had reached. They would not be returning to Trautenau, to their cherished former home. They could not safely remain in a disintegrating defenceless Czecho-Slovakia. At best, it offered temporary shelter, a respite, but with its borders breached and its dismemberment proceeding apace, it was surely only a matter of time before Hitler would absorb the remaining and wealthy Czech lands into his empire. They would then share the same fate as the Jews of Berlin and Vienna.

"So," Max resumed, "we have no choice. We will have to go. Somewhere."

Minna now joined the conversation.

"This arrived this morning when both of you were out," she said, pulling an envelope from a pocket in her apron, "it's a telegram from Arthur. It's addressed to you, Max," she added, passing it to him. "I haven't dared open it. I can't imagine what it might contain."

Max read aloud.

> *"No future here in Europe. Stop. Taking my chances in Palestine. Stop. Will write when possible. Stop. Love you. Miss you all. Stop. Arthur."*

Minna sat motionless for a moment and then looked away in a futile attempt to conceal the start of a gentle sobbing. Arthur had always been very close to his mother. Whilst Harry had been exploring foreign lands, Arthur had not strayed far from home until relatively recently. He had acquired some new friends in Moravia and earlier in the year had gone to join them and to find work near Brno. The prospect of prolonged separation had come without warning. Combined with the terrible events of the past few weeks it felt like a hammer blow for Minna. Max stared into a void, taken aback by the telegram.

"Palestine," mused Harry, taking his mother's hand, "it's a possibility, I suppose. Why not?"

"Not at my age," replied Max, "my days digging the dusty earth are behind me." Harry smiled to himself. He could not imagine Arthur toiling in the desert heat in barren fields and he certainly could not imagine his brother fired up with the pioneer spirit which seemed to inspire his more zealous Zionist friends.

"I didn't think Arthur had much time for Zionism," Harry said, "but times have changed; perhaps he has. Nothing is as it was."

"No," confirmed Max, "he didn't. There was a sudden passionate enthusiasm a few years ago for Zionism amongst some of the younger men and women. Organisations recruited potential volunteers for *Aliyah*, as they called it. They even ran training camps to prepare them. Some were religious, others weren't. Arthur went to a couple of meetings of the Zionist Club but that was the height of it, as far as we knew. It wasn't for him."

A few weeks ago Harry would have been surprised at his younger brother's decision but perhaps he had after all been influenced by his new friends as well as the dramatic events of the autumn. Arthur, the least religiously observant member of the family, had distanced himself from any overt adherence to Judaism. There were numerous strands in Zionism but as far as Harry knew, Arthur showed as little interest in politics as he had in religion. He did not share his father's anglophilia and his knowledge of English was rudimentary at best. Perhaps Palestine was a rational or only choice.

"Well, it looks as if we have all in our separate ways come to the same miserable conclusion," Harry said.

And with that, he rose from the table, taking a few paces towards the window to look out across the roof tops, glistening in a cold November drizzle which had descended on the small Czech frontier town. In the distance, lost behind the clouds, were the mountains of his former home and previous life. He did not expect to see them again for a long time but at that moment he felt neither loss nor longing.

"The *Riesengebirge*, the *Schneekoppe*, that's all in the past now," he said without sentimentality. Inside he did not feel as assertive and confident as his words sounded but he was filled with a new determination.

Dvůr Králové, November – December 1938

In the days and weeks that followed, they set about making the preparations to abandon an uncertain present for an uncertain future. The period of bewilderment after Munich was now replaced by bouts of hectic activity interspersed with agonising periods of waiting and enforced inactivity. As they discovered a new sense of purpose, they became painfully aware of how little they were in control of their fate. All energy was directed into escaping from the place they had for so long happily called home.

An early decision had been the most difficult: they would have to face the future not united as a family but separately, at least for the time being. Max's failure to secure a British passport for his sons lent Harry's preparations greater urgency. Whilst Max and Minna took some comfort in their British status, this only served to expose the extent to which Harry was vulnerable. He would have to forsake his current refuge in Dvůr Králové and find somewhere in the interior of the country, further away from the omnipresent threat of the Nazi authorities. His limited knowledge of Czech would immediately reveal him for what he was. Whatever steps he now took would be accompanied by risk. The interior would be safer than the border regions.

On Max's insistence, Harry had applied to enter the United Kingdom. He would have preferred France and above all Paris, which he adored and associated in his own mind with the carefree months he had enjoyed there a decade previously. He had even considered the United States where Sam, his mother's brother, had settled but that seemed so far away, so remote. Max had been less romantic and more severely practical, questioning how Harry might earn his living in France despite his fluent French. He undertook instead to write to friends in the textile business in Northern Ireland.

Max had visited Belfast over the years as a flax merchant and had even been instrumental in the purchase of looms for the local textile industry in Trautenau. Some of his acquaintances in Northern Ireland were connected to a major engineering enterprise which specialised in machinery for the linen industry. They were people of influence, Max assured his son. He would ask for help for Harry whose safety, he would tell them in no uncertain terms, was imperilled in the wake of the Nazi occupation. Tactfully he would omit any reference to betrayal at Munich.

Harry allowed himself to be persuaded. Max conceded that Belfast did not offer the same charms as Paris but, as it had been linen which had originally brought him to Trautenau, he told Harry, why should it not be linen which brought Harry the opportunity to discover a new world? Harry had replied, with a smile, that he had always thought it had been Minna who had been the reason for Max's arrival in the north-eastern Bohemian town. Max had quickly reassured him that Minna too was part of the reason. Harry wondered for his own brief amusement about the prospects of an Irish Minna.

Despite the unsuccessful outcome of his visit to Prague, Max had used the time at the Consulate to find out what conditions would apply for his sons to travel to England. He had drawn up a list of necessary documents and the requirement for guarantors to ensure that anyone arriving as a refugee would not be a cost to the British state. He had also discovered that there were opportunities in Northern Ireland where employment restrictions in force in England did not apply. Alternatively, passage might be granted to arrivals from Europe if it could be shown that they were in transit to another country prepared to grant permanent residence. Max now understood the vice consul's suggestion about trying South America; it had so greatly annoyed him and still rankled when it came up in a tense discussion.

"What was it they said at the Consulate?" asked Minna, "about countries which would give Harry a visa?"

"Are you seriously suggesting I should go to Argentina?" responded Harry, incredulously.

"It was Uruguay," Max added, not wanting to engage with the emerging argument.

"No," replied Minna, "I am just wondering whether one should not think a bit more about it. It may just be a possibility, at least for you and Arthur."

"I have thought about it and the answer is still no. Uruguay, Argentina, Cuba! And not the Dominican Republic either! You can forget all that nonsense, it's not for me!"

"Still," came Minna's gentle rejoinder, "thinking never hurts."

"It does!" Harry roared, "I can't stop thinking about this, this damned mess, about what's going to happen to us. I worry all the time! It makes me sick at heart!" He stood up abruptly and made for the door. Max and Minna were stunned by the outburst. It was years since they had witnessed one of Harry's flashes of temper, so familiar from his adolescence. The air and the rush of nicotine calmed Harry's frayed nerves as he paced aimlessly through the streets of the little town, turning the question over in his mind: am I really going to be a refugee? Thrown out? What does that mean, a refugee? When will all this end?

All three had struggled with coming to terms with what might lie ahead. The notion of packing their baggage, abandoning their home and fleeing belonged to the world of history or fiction, not modern, twentieth century Czechoslovakia in the heart of Europe. The image of the biblical Israelites, crossing the Red Sea with no more than they could carry on their backs, played vividly on Harry's mind, the fruit of decades of Passover evenings and the recitation of the most dramatic passages of the *Hagaddah*. In one sense, he now thought, it connected him and his family to an historical fate of Jews throughout time, forming part of the great Jewish continuum of exile and displacement. The very notion was absurd. It offered absolutely no comfort.

• • •

More practical matters commanded the family's attention.

Max had pursued access to his bank account in Trautenau. The occupying forces had moved swiftly to seize Jewish property and assets. The house in Reichstrasse was in the hands of the town's Gestapo. Max's bank account, in which he kept limited savings, had been frozen and then unfrozen as a British asset and he had transferred as much as he could to a bank account in Dvůr Králové, where he could draw on it to support their existence there.

Harry's position was more complicated. The special currency protection unit of the SS had on arrival seized all Jewish accounts in Reichenberg. He was dependent on his father. As a Czechoslovak citizen and a Jew who had fled the Reich, Harry had little prospect of persuading the authorities to release his savings. Even trying to recover any money at this volatile moment would involve disclosure of his current address. This, an acquaintance had advised him, was not a wise step. Safety now lay in anonymity.

Max had thrown himself energetically into the task of trying to recover as much of his moveable property as he could, arguing that His Majesty would be gravely displeased to learn of the difficulties experienced by his loyal subject in faraway Czecho-Slovakia. Max normally derived some pleasure from jousting by correspondence with bureaucracy. Now, he had lost all appetite for such pleasure-seeking. He could not tell and nor did he much care whether, after months of wrangling, it was his status as a British subject that had finally persuaded the authorities in Trautenau. A lorry loaded with furniture and other domestic goods, some books and paintings, had rattled into Dvůr Králové. Max would arrange for the goods to be safely stored in the yard of Georg Hammerschlag's transport and freight business, awaiting his further instructions.

In the meantime Harry would go to Prague to prepare to leave and to seek a beneficiary and a safe haven in a foreign country.

HARRY 1935: Everything to look forward to

Dvůr Králové, February 1939

The dreaded moment arrived. On a freezing cold day in early February Max and Minna accompanied Harry to the bus for Prague, knowing that separation was necessary and potentially indefinite. Harry promised faithfully to write as often as he could. It might take a few weeks to make the final arrangements to travel to England. You could never be sure. There were so many papers and stamps needed just for one single journey. He would await his parents in London.

The previous day a short letter, the first in two months, had arrived from Arthur; he was with friends near Timisoara in Romania, in good health and spirits. He had found some temporary work in a chocolate factory and was earning enough money to continue his journey soon, hoping to reach Constanza on the Black Sea within a few weeks when the weather got warmer. From there he planned to travel by ship to Istanbul and beyond to Palestine, legally or otherwise. There was no further detail other than that he had lost a little bit of weight and that he missed his mother's cooking.

Harry duly bade farewell to his parents. After a long embrace he climbed aboard the bus to take him on his first reluctant step into the unknown. He had originally packed two very bulky suitcases. They were old companions, Harry thought, as he contemplated the array of brightly coloured stickers, testimony to the many places - Florence, Vienna, La Spezia, Rome, Paris – he and his cases had visited in happier times. In those days a prosperous young gentleman travelled with a variety of shoes, shirts and suits appropriate for all encounters and occasions. With an amused smile he recalled the good-natured tussles with his mother about her insistence on additional underwear, socks, scarves and gloves. He had been young then, carefree, embarking on adventures, confident and full of optimism. It had been an age of innocence. Now he felt darkly anxious.

In the end he had decided that just a single case would make him less conspicuous. In his spare hand he clutched his leather briefcase containing all the important documents he needed. He would keep it with him at all times. To all intents and purposes, he appeared to be an ordinary local businessman on a routine business trip to the capital. He was wearing a hat, scarf and gloves and smart well-polished shoes. His mother was pleased that he looked respectable. Aware of the finality of the moment, Harry had other matters on his mind.

•••

As the bus slowly made its way south towards the capital his thoughts drifted in an uncontrolled way from his happy childhood and student years to a vague, anxiety-laden future. He thought about Arthur. Where might he be at this very moment? Would he also soon be on a bus or a boat taking him into the unknown? How long would he remain in Timisoara? Was he safe? When would they see each other again?

Did Arthur share Harry's anxiety or was his enviably optimistic disposition, something he had inherited from his father, shining through? Only two years younger, Arthur had been his closest companion in early childhood but soon the different natures of the brothers had become apparent. As Harry recalled, Arthur did not share his love of books nor his studiousness. He was always much happier playing in the garden or the woods nearby, climbing trees or making dens, whilst Harry immersed himself in a good story.

Harry smiled to himself as he remembered the day Arthur had come home, bursting with excited pride and carrying a rabbit, still alive, which he had managed to catch. Their mother had been horrified and insisted he release the creature back into the wild. Arthur had been upset but had complied. Later his father had told them all a story of how, during the Boer War, he had, out of necessity, trapped various small animals, including rabbits, which he had cooked over an open wood fire. Arthur had derived some comfort from his father's exploits; Harry suspected that his father had embellished the tale, which he thought owed something to nineteenth century stories he had once read at school.

Harry's memories of the later adolescent years and beyond were more uncomfortable. Arthur had not followed his older brother to the grammar school but attended a technical school instead. Although nothing was ever stated explicitly, Harry knew that Arthur felt that he was, if not exactly a failure, then certainly a disappointment to his parents, especially to his father. When Harry had been dispatched proudly to study at the prestigious Hochschule in Vienna, Arthur had joylessly entered the family business as an apprentice flax merchant. He had worked conscientiously but without conviction or enthusiasm. A visit to his student older brother in Vienna had not been a success; Harry's new university friends inhabited a different world and Harry had afterwards agreed with Arthur when he had complained miserably that they had been condescending towards him.

ARTHUR

And then the rift had occurred.

Now, years after the event, Harry still reproached himself. Caught between filial demands from his parents and fraternal loyalty, he had caved in and played the role of the obedient son. Even now it troubled his conscience. Arthur could be strong-willed and independent-minded. Whereas Harry was instinctively conformist, Arthur had a rebellious streak. This had extended to friendships he struck up with members of both sexes, inside the small Jewish community and outside as well.

Arthur had already turned twenty-one at the time and felt he had the right to explore relationships as he saw fit. One particular friendship with a young woman a few years older, had raised eyebrows and led to unflattering comments from some of the stalwarts of the Jewish community whom Max and Minna encountered every Saturday after the service at the synagogue. The woman in question was not Jewish; her father was Czech, a brewery-worker, her mother German and a seamstress. She had a room in town and no longer lived at home. It had been noticed that she and Arthur were spending a great deal of time together including long weekends hiking in the mountains. The affair was taking on the characteristics of a more solid, potentially permanent relationship. Max and Minna confided to Harry that they felt alarmed. The woman was not of their faith nor social standing and in their opinion barely respectable. Harry had been asked to talk seriously with Arthur about his parents' concerns and their disapproval of how he was behaving. They would not be happy to see the friendship evolve further into something more enduring. Harry did not want to dwell on the details. It had become a deeply painful episode.

The conversation between the brothers had been disastrous. Harry knew he had been clumsy in how he broached the matter but the explosion of anger and resentment from Arthur had taken him aback. In the end Arthur and the young woman had drifted apart and gone their separate ways. Harry felt that he had been caught in an impossible position.

No matter how analytical he was retrospectively, no matter how carefully he considered his dilemma, he could not overcome a sense of shame about his own conduct. Arthur had the right to live his own life. No-one had ever suggested improprieties to Harry as he pursued several relationships of his own, away from home and the censorious eyes of his parents. It had taken years to repair the damage. Had Arthur ever truly forgiven him for his intervention? Harry ardently hoped so but remained uncertain. Had he not done enough since then to earn or win back his brother's trust? And yet, as he journeyed now into a perilous world, just as somewhere else in Europe, his brother was embarked on a parallel venture, Harry yearned for nothing more than to be close to Arthur, to be sitting next to him in a coffee house or enjoying a game of tennis or climbing the Schneekoppe, as they had done so often in more innocent times. He wanted to know that they had been reconciled. The next time the two brothers were reunited, he would be candid about how he now viewed his previous actions. He would try to finally resolve the matter. It might be awkward, but it had to be done. He would ask for forgiveness if that was what was required.

•••

When Harry awoke his bus was pulling into Florenc bus-station in the centre of Prague. There was snow on the ground; the city looked grey, forbidding, hostile. He knew the capital well; it was barely 100 kilometres from his point of departure, but he now felt a long way from home. Gone was the vertiginous thrill of arriving in and exploring other great cities. Instead, an unpleasant sensation, a gloomy foreboding and unease gripped him. He was approaching a point of no return. And he was alone.

3.
ADRIFT

Prague, February 1939

And so in February 1939, approaching his thirtieth birthday, Harry found himself in Prague to complete the final preparations for his departure for England. Max's contacts and good name had in the end had some positive effect. The question of acquiring a British passport had never again been mentioned but the Passport Control Office at the Consulate had been prepared to issue a travel document granting Leon Harry Lewy permission to enter the United Kingdom on a temporary basis. From Vienna where he was now stationed, Captain Taylor's intervention on behalf of his old friend had been sufficient. Max had procured a letter of sponsorship through his business connections in Belfast. There were still formalities to undertake: the purchase of a one-way transit train ticket through the Reich, permission to enter and travel through the Netherlands and a boat ticket for the crossing from Hook of Holland to Harwich, an affidavit from the American authorities to confirm that he was intending to apply for a visa to travel onwards to the USA where he had an uncle in

New Jersey. All arrangements were hedged around with bureaucracy but the task of drawing them together would be less complicated now that he was in the capital. There was also the delicate matter of financial inducements, should they be necessary.

Harry had no illusions. There were indeed many individual Czechs sympathetic to his plight and that of his fellow refugees from the Sudetenland but, by contrast, the hostility of the new government was unmistakable. Administrative measures, including financial controls, limited his room for manoeuvre. The authorities were keenly alert to the opportunity to get their hands on Jewish assets and were making life difficult and potentially dangerous, especially for the German-speaking Jews from the ceded territories who, like all Germans, were unwelcome and viewed with suspicion. Police patrols were on the look-out for anyone whose papers might not be in order or who was otherwise unfortunate enough to draw attention to himself. Hotels, it was rumoured, were a particular trap and needed to be avoided. Single young men without a gainful occupation were an obvious target. Random checks in the street added to the constant need to be on one's guard.

Heinz, a friend from childhood who now lived in Prague, met Harry at Florenc. The friends exchanged handshakes and embraced.

"Come with me, Harry," Heinz said quietly, "I need to explain to you how things work here." Taking his case, Heinz guided Harry out of the busy bus station and into the narrow streets leading towards the Old Town. Over a coffee and a pastry in an inconspicuous café, Heinz set out what he called the basic rules.

"Above all else, do not draw attention to yourself! How you dress, where you go, who you meet, what you say. Just merge into the background."

"I know," Harry replied, "but how?"

"That's not so easy. For a start, avoid speaking German. Best say nothing, if you can; and don't trust anyone. You never know who you are dealing with."

"If you need money," Heinz continued, " be sure only to withdraw small amounts from the bank. Larger transactions will immediately draw attention to you. That could spell danger."

"But I have to collect documents, go to the British Consulate, buy tickets. I have to have somewhere to live until I get permission to travel to Britain. It could be weeks, months."

"I know," said Heinz, "it's the same for me, for all of us. But remember, Prague has changed. The government is after us, that's bad enough but everyone fears the Germans will invade and do what they did in Austria last year. You have to remain out of sight."

"I can't just disappear," Harry remonstrated.

"You can and you will," Heinz replied sharply. " Avoid public parks, anywhere where a single man without anything to do might stand out. Only last week the police rounded up a group of men and shipped them off to a labour camp, just like that. These are dangerous times."

On Heinz's advice Harry decided to find a private room to rent away from the centre of the city. He would avoid registering with the Prague authorities as required, preferring instead to take the risk, if challenged, of giving his address in Dvůr Králové. If anyone there came looking for him, his parents would simply say he was away for a few days. Thus he entered an unaccustomed twilight world of a clandestine existence in which he would learn to become increasingly invisible until he effectively ceased to exist.

An acquaintance of Heinz's, already used to living in the shadows, gave him a name and address where he might safely stay whilst awaiting clearance to travel. Maria Fischlová lived on the fourth floor of a tenement block in Žižkov, an insalubrious district outside the city centre but within walking distance of the main railway station. She had a small room which she rented to temporary guests, provided they would cause her no trouble. Respectable single gentlemen like Dr Lewy were ideal. She asked no questions and did not expect any in return. The rent was affordable but had to be paid on time. She would provide a cup of coffee in the morning and a bed at night. Once a week she would do the washing and ironing for a few crowns extra. It was not the lifestyle to which Harry had been used but he was content. He could live out of a suitcase and out of sight. It was all he needed for what he expected to be a short stay.

Žižkov was notorious, Harry had been told. Its tightly packed tenements were home to a section of Prague's working class but also to many who were happier living their lives away from the gaze of the authorities. The police rarely ventured into the heart of the area and when they did, only for as short a time as necessary. Maria Fischlová worked night shifts. Harry thought she cleaned trams and trains but he did not enquire and she did not volunteer such details. Discretion provided protection. She had lent Harry a coat inherited from a previous occupant of the room. Harry's own elegant and fashionably long leather overcoat, a reminder of better times, would immediately stand out on the streets and attract unwanted attention, she cautioned him; being conspicuous was precisely the kind of thing Heinz had warned against. His newly acquired shabby replacement helped him merge into the generally down-at-heel appearance of the locals when he needed to venture out. Harry thought fleetingly of his mother who would be appalled at his appearance; he was grimly amused but it was a small compromise.

After several weeks of concentrated effort and patience, combined with periods of inactivity, he had at last assembled all the papers he needed to purchase his one-way train ticket out of the country. He would depart from Wilson station on Tuesday 28 March, travel across Germany and into the Netherlands, taking the ferry from Hook of Holland to Harwich. He would be in England before the end of March or early April at the latest. All that remained was to bide his time, staying out of view, on his own, waiting to bid his unhappy homeland farewell and embark on a journey into the unknown. Return was not permitted. It was an adventure he had never wished upon himself.

Prague, February to March 1939

"Harry, Harry Lewy!"

Harry froze. He did not want to be recognised, here in the street or anywhere else. Anonymity meant safety. For a moment he could not place the familiar voice but turning round, he immediately knew the woman who had hailed him. Her delight was evident.

"What are you doing here in Prague?"

"I'm in the process of leaving," he replied drily, "I'm going to England."

"Oh, that's wonderful!" she exclaimed, then correcting herself, "I mean, how terribly sad, how awful. On your own?"

It was almost three years since Harry had last seen Helly. A great deal had happened in the intervening time. She must have completed her studies, he assumed. He had heard that she had got married.

"How is your mother?", he enquired. He had been very fond of Mrs Katz and the enquiry was as genuine as it was courteous.

"How are any of us?" Helly answered, "she's fine, given the circumstances."

"Where are you staying?" she enquired.

"Oh, I've found a little place in Žižkov," he replied, anticipating her reaction.

"Hmmm, Žižkov, I see."

He volunteered no further details and she left the matter there.

For a time, Helly and Harry had been close to each other and had enjoyed many happy hours together, on skis in the mountains, walking, talking, thinking perhaps of the future. He had missed her passion for life, her energy and ambition; she, for her part, had missed his kindness, his wit and his learning. Seeing her again by chance at this moment filled him with sadness but also reminded him of the affection for her he had never really lost, even after they had drifted apart. It was wholly typical, he thought, that this encounter should be taking place outside a bookshop. How many hours had they spent together talking about books?

"Could I invite you to come round for a coffee and a chat?" she asked, "it would be much nicer than standing here in the street in the cold. And I can introduce you to Paul. You'll like him."

Her smile exuded warmth. He wondered for a moment whether she might even offer him a bed in their flat if they had the space.

Her mother would make one of her delicious cakes, Helly insisted, and they could reminisce about old and better times, exchange news of old acquaintances and friends. Helly did not really need to insist. The invitation was enticing and after weeks avoiding almost all human contact, Harry welcomed the prospect of company and accepted readily.

Prague, 14 March 1939

On the evening of Tuesday 14 March, Maria Fischlová announced that she would not be going to work that night. Earlier in the day Harry had noticed a slip of paper pushed under the door of her flat but had thought nothing of it and had not mentioned it.

"There's all sorts of stories flying around: unrest, spies everywhere, German troop movements. Safer to stay put," was all she offered by way of explanation.

There were plenty of rumours in the capital in mid-March 1939.

A new crisis was brewing. Snatches of conversation were exchanged at street corners. Slovakia had finally declared itself independent; Sub-Carpathian Ruthenia on the far eastern fringes of the former republic had swiftly followed suit. Everyone knew that the existence of the rump state of Czecho-Slovakia was being terminated, as had long been anticipated. To widespread consternation, Radio Prague had informed the expectant citizens of the dying republic that their ageing president, Emil Hácha, had travelled to Berlin that afternoon to see the Führer. The Czech fascists, who shared so much with their German counterparts, were increasingly emboldened. The Government had passed an Enabling Act which allowed it to rule by decree.

Earlier, in January, the Communist Party had been banned, a measure which had not greatly troubled Harry in practice although he wondered about the general principle. However, a new measure enacted on 2 March presented a much more immediate threat. The new law against vagrancy allowed the authorities to detain all men over the age of 18 who were unemployed and send them to the recently established state-run forced labour camps. Harry had not to that point ever considered himself to be a vagrant. He could not imagine himself as some kind of *clochard*, such as he knew from Paris, but when he thought about it, that was exactly what he was now being reduced to. If stopped in the street by anyone in a uniform and asked his business and where he worked, he was utterly unarmed. Unemployed thirty-year-old Dr Harry Lewy fulfilled the criteria to be considered a vagrant and as such liable to peremptory detention and removal to a labour camp. By yet another twist of the screw his mere existence was further endangered. And now Mrs Fischlová, too, was choosing to stay out of sight, at least on this evening, as if the danger which surrounded him might envelop her too.

He thought fondly of the recent encounter with Helly outside a bookshop where he had gone, despite the risks, to find some new reading material to help him pass the time. He had wanted to read Joseph Roth's popular family saga, *Radetzky March*, but had not found the time. The decline of Austria-Hungary seemed an apposite theme. He had always enjoyed Roth's stories. He had time to kill.

He had gladly accepted her invitation and had spent a pleasant couple of hours with her and her husband, Paul. Her mother had been as warm and animated as always all those years ago in Trautenau when he had been a welcome and frequent guest at the Katz family home above their shop. And Mrs Katz had, as anticipated, baked a wonderful cake. Their upbeat conversation had ranged far and wide despite the ominous circumstances of their encounter. That evening too already belonged to a distant time.

•••

Although he had been a "guest" for over a month, he had exchanged few words with Mrs Fischlová beyond the necessary conversation between lodger and landlady and occasional items of news. Clearly she knew about his situation; he had told her about his intended date of departure and ultimate destination. She understood discretion and his need to remain anonymous, even to the extent of avoiding contact with the other residents on the fourth-floor landing of the grimy tenement. For all he knew, there might be another gentleman also in transit living next door. On the other hand, it was equally possible that fascist activists also lived in the block. Maria Fischlová might have been about fifty, more or less the same age as his mother. She looked tired when she peered earnestly at him from behind her wire rimmed spectacles. They lent her the air of an intellectual, Harry thought, as he also reflected on how little he knew about his landlady. Her hair was greying beneath her headscarf and she habitually wore an apron at home. Unlike many Czechs she seemed equally at home in German as in her native language. Perhaps she had not spent her entire life cleaning trams and buses at night. Had he been recommended to her because she was part of an organisation, he wondered; was she a Communist, a Zionist perhaps? Only once had she given any indication of political affiliation when she had started a sentence with the words "Comrade Stalin says..." but then she had halted abruptly and changed the subject.

"I'll stay in tonight", she said, "and we'll see how matters stand in the morning. I'll pick up your cigarettes and the newspaper for you. You just stay put."

Prague, Wednesday 15 March 1939

As Harry was subsequently to find out from Mrs. Fischlová, events developed rapidly that night. President Hácha's meeting with Hitler in Berlin resulted in a radio announcement: he was placing the fate of Bohemia and Moravia, all that remained of Czechoslovakia, in the hands of and under the protection of the German leader.

Before dawn, units of the *Wehrmacht* began to advance on Prague from four directions, meeting no resistance on the icy roads or in the snowy skies. By nine in the morning, Prague was under German occupation. Wild rejoicing on the part of the city's German population and in particular the students at Prague's German University was matched by sullen shock and distress amongst the Czech majority. Later in the evening of 15 March Hitler arrived at the Castle, *Hradschin* to the Germans, *Hradčany* to the Czechs, to savour his spectacular triumph. Neither the British nor the French raised a finger. The *Protektorat von Böhmen und Mähren*, the Protectorate of Bohemia and Moravia, had come into existence. How long it would endure no-one knew.

German troops occupy Prague Castle, the seat of Government, 15 March 1939

The Germans moved swiftly and efficiently to assert control over their latest acquisition. They arrived prepared and well informed. Individuals, in particular, political opponents and their organisations, mostly socialists, communists and trade unionists, and including artists, writers and intellectuals in exile from Germany or Austria and the Sudetenland, were immediate targets. And of course, Jews. Foreign embassies, including the British Embassy on Thunovská, were besieged by panic-stricken, terrified crowds desperate to get away. Within days a number of radio stations, theatres and newspapers had fallen silent. Specialist German security units had begun the task of the systematic seizure of prominent Jews and Jewish assets.

•••

Harry did not venture beyond Mrs Fischlová's flat from that day, 15 March 1939, until the time came for him to make his way carefully to the railway station. As promised, Mrs Fischlová kept him supplied with cigarettes but the *Prager Tagblatt* she brought him on the morning after the invasion was the last edition of that venerable newspaper he ever read. For decades, the newspaper of choice for Prague's liberal-minded German-speaking intelligentsia, the *Tagblatt* had been one of the doughtiest defenders of the First Republic and Masaryk's humanist ideals. Harry recalled that journalists fleeing from the Reich had found a welcome in its pages and been amongst its liveliest and most challenging contributors.

Harry looked in disbelief at the front page, dominated by the news of the occupation. "*With History. Ancient Reich lands German once again!*" proclaimed the headlines in traditional Gothic typescript. The editors had been tipped off in good time. What shocked and hurt Harry, already growing immune to new and terrible events, was the editorial greeting the invasion, which concluded with "*Heil Hitler!*" He remembered vividly the editorial which had so impressed him months previously in the coffee house in Dvůr Králové. He folded the paper and put it to one side. On this day he would not follow his routine of reading every word, including the advertisements, sports news, weather information and death notices. Two words had sufficed. Another betrayal. He felt heart-broken. Another light extinguished. He was counting the days.

Nazi parade down Wenceslas Square, Prague, Protectorate of Bohemia and Moravia

Prague, Tuesday 28 March 1939

Harry slept badly the night before he was due to depart.

The full magnitude of the step he was about to undertake overawed him. All bonds would be broken, at least for the foreseeable future.

When would he be reunited with his parents or Arthur? Was Arthur too being forced to lie low? Was he also in constant danger? So much had happened since leaving Dvůr Králové. Was there anything he could do to help his brother? No, he concluded miserably, they were each on their own.

He did not dream, as far as he could recall but seemed to rehearse in his mind troubling encounters with threatening officials, sinister figures in dark uniforms and suspicious fellow passengers on the journey which lay ahead. Before that he would have to make his way to the station. He wrote a brief note to his parents, informing them that he was on the point of departure and that he would contact them again once he had reached his destination. He had not heard from the 'King at the Round Table', he added obliquely, knowing his parents would instantly recognise the family code. He did not sign the note nor give an address. He would ask Mrs Fischlová to post it the day after his train had departed.

By the time Mrs Fischlová knocked on his bedroom door with a coffee in hand, he had been awake for several hours. He had shaved carefully and was dressed. He had acquired a second small battered suitcase since his original departure from Dvůr Králové. Mrs Fischlová had explained that one of her previous gentlemen, as she put it delicately, had left it behind at the last moment. It was into these two cases, small and light enough for him to carry as hand luggage, that he now packed the remains of his past life and the sparse necessities for his future existence. His briefcase with its extended strap would slip over his shoulder so that he would not be parted from its precious contents at any time. He had heard stories of travellers in similar circumstances stitching valuables or foreign currency into garments, opening hems to conceal valuables certain to be confiscated or just stolen by vigilant guards and opportunists at border crossings. Cautious and conformist by nature, Harry had decided against such attempts to circumvent the regulations.

The German authorities had published a list of items which it was forbidden to remove from the country. Harry permitted himself a wry smile at the fantasy of the precious manuscripts and oil paintings he would have to leave behind before returning brusquely to the reality that he was practically penniless and that the total of his wealth and possessions fitted into two cases. For a fleeting instant, a few lines of his beloved Heine ran through his head as he remembered the poet describing an encounter with customs officials as he had crossed into Prussia. The officials had rummaged in his luggage looking for forbidden goods to confiscate; Heine had subsequently mocked them in his poem. The most valuable item, the most dangerous contraband, was safely stored in his head, away from prying eyes. Harry accepted that his own head contained no more than a bundle of jumbled thoughts and confused emotions, of which trepidation was the most dominant. The prospect of his German journey daunted him. Had he space for the volume of selected Heine poems which had been his constant companion for many years? No, he decided, they were a provocation for any semi-literate but hostile official who might choose to open his case. He would leave the poems with Mrs Fischlová and tell her with a feigned jauntiness that she should look after it. He would be back one day to collect it.

"May I come in?" she asked.

In the six weeks Harry had lived there she had not once asked to bring in his morning coffee, which she had always left by the door. Normally she would retreat to her bedroom to sleep, having completed her night shift and provided for her lodger, as prescribed in the agreement they had made with each other.

"Yes, of course," Harry replied. He sat on the narrow bed as she entered carrying not the usual cup and saucer but a tray with a pot, two cups and some breakfast goods which comprised bread rolls, butter and a small dish of red jam. She placed the tray on the small table, the only luxury item in Harry's room. Harry barely concealed his surprise but her company was welcome.

"So you're ready?" she enquired, "everything packed?"

He nodded.

"There are just a couple of things I wanted to go over before you leave," she said.

"Please can you check that you leave nothing behind in the room. When you've gone, I will prepare the room for another guest who is due here soon. There must be no trace of anything to indicate you were ever here."

Harry was vaguely amused by this overt cloak and dagger drama despite having spent so long being invisible.

"No, of course not," he replied, "all my worldly possessions are in my cases, with the exception of two pairs of socks which are full of holes, some back numbers of the *Prager Tagblatt* and this little book of poems by Heine which I would like you to have."

"That's very kind," she said, "I used to enjoy poetry."

"The other thing to give you is the overcoat you lent me when I arrived. I don't think I'll need it any more now."

"Yes you will," she cut in firmly, "you have to get to the station, remember. The same rules apply. As inconspicuous as possible. Your leather coat is far too elegant for around here. You won't get two steps before some troublemaker will be asking who the gent is in the smart coat. We've been through this before." She was no longer making conversation but giving clear unequivocal instructions. "I will walk with you to the station."

"Really, Mrs Fischlová, that's very kind, but there is no need. It's fifteen, maybe twenty minutes' walk. I can easily find the way."

"And straight into the grateful arms of the police or the Gestapo," she countered. "A man and a woman going to the station with suitcases look a bit more normal these days than a single young man on his own. Four eyes are better than two. I'm coming with you, as far as the station entrance. Then you're on your own."

"That's very kind," replied Harry again. He felt protected by her decisiveness, suspecting she was following a practised routine. It was not his place to enquire. If it helped him embark safely on his journey, he was happy to comply with her directives.

•••

The moment to leave arrived. Harry's cases stood ready by the door.

"Here," she said, "put these in your briefcase. You've a long journey in front of you". She handed him a packet. "A couple of sandwiches, nothing fancy, and a bar of chocolate. And cigarettes, you'll need these, won't you?"

Harry was touched by this unexpected and unprompted kindness but before he could find any suitable words, she was already outside on the landing, one suitcase in hand. "Come on, now," she commanded, as she looked left and right before descending the staircase into the courtyard and out through the heavy bolted wooden door into the street. It was the first time since the invasion that Harry had been outside the tenement. The cool fresh morning air struck him and he allowed himself the luxury of a deep breath, savouring its novelty, before following her towards Husitská, the main road which led down from Žižkov towards the station.

It was an unremarkable spring morning. Leaves were already appearing on the trees; people were going about their daily business. Trams rattled by, their bells ringing as they approached the frequent stops where passengers alighted or climbed on. The normality of it all clashed violently with the emotions coursing through Harry's whole being. Here were people getting on calmly with their ordinary banal lives, doing what they did every day, day after day, month after month and here was he, Dr Leon Harry Lewy, on the threshold of the absurd abnormality of overturning everything he had ever known, about to plunge into whatever awaited him, uncertain of where he might wash up. Exterior calm sat uncomfortably with inner uproar.

Mrs Fischlová led the way as they turned left into Španělská and continued downhill towards the front of the station. He could hear the station announcements and the familiar sounds of trains arriving and departing. And then, as they approached the main entrance it struck him how everything was different, wrong, disturbing. Everywhere, from the impressive buildings and the lampposts, hung huge banners in brilliant red, in the middle of which stood a black swastika on a white roundel. The more he looked, the more he realised that there were not just a few of the symbols of Nazism but hundreds, to right and left, and that the trams too sported little flags where the swastika had been placed side by side with miniature Czech flags. Then two open-backed tenders drove past with steel-helmeted soldiers in the uniform of the occupying *Wehrmacht* sitting bolt upright, rifles between their knees, pointing upwards. Nobody seemed to notice but Harry wanted to stand and stare, to absorb what he was witnessing. Mrs Fischlová pressed on resolutely and he had to quicken his pace to keep up with her. In the preceding ten days or so she had already had ample opportunity to absorb the changes in her home city and to become aware of new dangers in the streets. For Harry, the first visual impact of the occupation was profound. If he had ever for an instant hesitated about whether he was embarking on the right course of action, the scene that greeted him now confirmed his decision. If he had been tempted to think he was over-dramatising the dangers he faced, all such thoughts now dissipated. Contemplating this alien landscape he knew he was an outcast here. Until this point, the occupation of Prague had been something of which he had heard, read and imagined but not witnessed directly from the relative security of his shelter. Confronted with the enormity of the physical reality of the *Protektorat*, he shivered, inwardly trembling. They had reached the forecourt of the station.

"This is where we say goodbye," declared Mrs Fischlová, "I wish you a safe journey and every good fortune. Do not forget us, Dr Lewy!"

She proffered her hand in parting, turned and disappeared down the steps in front of the station, merging rapidly into the crowd of pedestrians heading away from the station in the direction of the museum and Wenceslas Square. Harry had prepared a short speech of thanks in his mind, no more than a sentence or so of gratitude for the monosyllabic woman who had sheltered him but she was gone before he could utter a word. He turned to face the entrance and the giant red banners draped down its imposing façade. Feeling exposed as never before, he walked slowly towards the main doors as if everyone knew his business and was looking at him, scrutinising this odd figure lugging his suitcases towards the trains.

•••

"Your papers!" demanded an official voice as he entered the main hall. Harry had rehearsed this moment many times in his mind in recent days. He would remain impassive and say as little as possible. He produced his Czechoslovak personal identity card which was still regarded as valid proof of who he was.

"Hmmm, Lewy?" enquired the official. Harry nodded. Was the official specifically drawing attention to his obviously Jewish name or just undertaking a routine confirmation that the bearer of the document matched the name on the card?

"Destination?"

"Hook of Holland via Frankfurt and Cologne, then London," replied Harry, trying to sound as if this was a familiar, routine journey he had made many times before.

"Platform Four," said the official, indicating where Harry should go. "Make sure you have all your documents ready for inspection, over there, where the big queue is. They'll want you to open your suitcases as well."

"Thank you," replied Harry curtly.

"Have a pleasant journey," answered the official and then with just the faintest hint of a smile creasing his face, "Good luck, Dr Lewy."

Harry threaded his way through the crowds milling around in the hall and joined the less than orderly queue which had already assembled at the entrance to the platform. A large trestle table formed a barrier behind which sat two uniformed German officers and a civilian. Behind them guarding access to the platform stood two more German soldiers; to either side Harry noticed one or two additional figures, stereotypical images of plain clothes policemen, as if borrowed directly from the local cinema. The queue moved slowly forward. From time to time the stereotypes identified individual travellers for further questioning. Seemingly random suitcases, usually the bigger ones, were selected for detailed inspection which entailed rough rummaging or tipping out of contents on the floor of the station, a visible humiliation. Occasionally, an item would be removed. Distraught men and women were then left to repack the scattered contents of their cases under the disparaging gaze of officials. The intended effect was all too obvious, Harry thought. And then it was his turn.

"Destination?"

Harry repeated the answer he had already given on arrival at the station.

"Documents," demanded the Czech civilian. "Passport first, then police clearance papers, currency declaration, suitcase contents list, dated Reich transit documents, entrance papers for Holland, train tickets, seat reservation!"

Harry complied. He produced his Czechoslovak passport, the passport he had used for years, issued in Prague for a country which no longer existed. It bore all the relevant stamps he had painstakingly accumulated: permission to enter the German Reich on a one-way journey with return forbidden, with a validity of three days from the beginning of the journey on 28 March to its conclusion. On the facing page was permission to enter the Netherlands on a one-way only transit visa; overleaf, permission to enter the United Kingdom. He laid on the table the statement indicating that he had no police record and that as there were no matters outstanding, he had permission to leave the country. Perhaps they want to see my Permission to Breathe statement, Harry thought to himself but this was not the moment for facetiousness. He remained silent as all his papers were scrutinised and each in turn was adorned with a fresh stamp bearing a small swastika alongside the place and date.

"Open your cases, Lewy!"

Harry did as instructed.

"List of contents!"

He presented the carefully hand-written list: two pairs of shoes, one black, one brown, two suits, one brown, one dark blue and three-piece, one Czech, one Italian. Three shirts, two cotton, one linen, three ties, all silk. Two sets of cufflinks, silver. The list went on. It was, Harry thought, no more than a commercial traveller going on a business trip for a week or so, might take with him. There was nothing controversial. The officials appeared to concur.

"Valuables: gold, diamonds, works of art, stamp collections, large denomination currency?" barked one of the German officers, who had been supervising the proceedings.

Harry smiled politely. "No, nothing of that kind."

"Forbidden materials, enemy propaganda, books, weapons?"

Harry had thought long and hard about books. Most of what he considered worth reading was now banned in Germany but he would be in transit. The German authorities would not make a fuss, he hoped. He would take a few books and if the worst came to the worst, they would be confiscated.

"I have a few books with me, just for private use," he answered.

"Take them out!"

So Harry fished out his small selection and began to stack them on the table: *Selected Nineteenth Century German Poetry*, Dickens' *Tale of Two Cities*, Ignazio Silone's *Fontamara*, in Italian, Zola's *Thérèse Raquin* in French and Stefan Zweig's *Marie Antionette*. It was an eclectic collection, chosen with care and reflecting Harry's broad tastes and interests.

"And there we have it, gentlemen," sneered one of the two Germans seated next to the Czech official at the table, addressing his colleague as he pointed to the books, "the rootless, cosmopolitan, Jewish intellectual." He paused. "Pack them back in your case." And then turning to his companion, he added, "who cares what this damned Jew reads!"

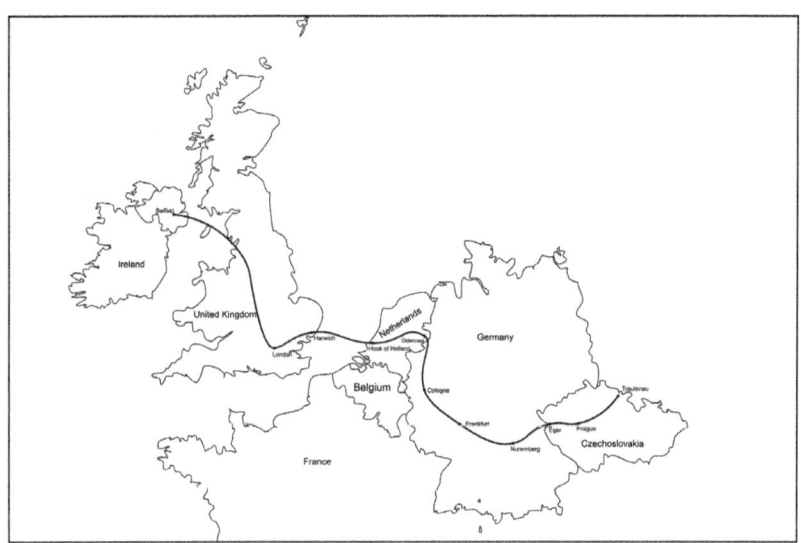

Harry's journey to safety and freedom

4.
TRANSIT

And then Harry was through the barrier to the platform, making his way to his carriage. The compartment was empty when he arrived. He stowed his two cases in the luggage rack above his head and took his seat in the corner by the window. He felt exhausted, as if he had been working hard all day. It was less than two hours since he had left the tenement. He lit a cigarette and gazed out of the window, hoping that his fellow passengers who would shortly fill the compartment, were not of the intrusive compulsive talker sort one sometimes encountered on a journey. He had determined to keep himself to himself as much as he could. It was nobody's concern where he was going and why. His mind wandered to the sandwiches Mrs Fischlová had prepared for him and the chocolate bar lying in his briefcase. He decided that he had better keep them for the long journey ahead. He had no idea if and when he might next get something to eat or drink and how far the few Reichmarks he had been permitted to purchase at the bank would go. He fell into a fitful snooze.

The shrill blast of a whistle roused him from his sleep. The compartment was full. Two youngish couples and an elderly gentleman were engaged in animated discussion. All were speaking German; one couple had the unmistakable accent of the northern Sudetenland. He could not be certain but he suspected that he might not be the sole passenger with a one-way ticket. The massive locomotive had steamed up and the train gradually began to pull out of the station. As a child he had been fascinated by the giant engines which hauled trains across Europe. Innocent times, he reflected. A few minutes later, they were crossing the river and heading west towards Eger and the former German border.

The journey as far as Eger proved surprisingly uneventful. Now fully incorporated into the Reich to which it had "returned", Eger was no longer truly a border town. The formalities completed at Wilson station had been sufficient for the time being. Shortly after departure there had been the usual ticket inspection to ensure that passengers were indeed seated in their reserved places. Apart from a brief visit to the toilet at the end of the corridor, Harry remained ensconced in his seat, staring fixedly out of the window. From time to time his eyelids became heavy in the warm atmosphere of the full compartment as he sank into a shallow slumber. His fellow passengers seemingly accepted that the solitary young man in the corner was not the talkative type. A couple of hours later, as the train was pulling into Eger station, where it would pick up additional passengers, the elderly man sitting opposite him asked suddenly, addressing Harry directly:

"Is the gentleman going far?"

"Hook of Holland," Harry replied, offering no further information.

"Oh, so are we," said one of the two young women. The single older man chipped in that he too was making for the Netherlands but was planning to change trains and travel to Amsterdam where he had friends.

"We're going as far as Nuremberg," the other woman volunteered. "My husband is taking up a new job, aren't you, darling? It's a big promotion. Senior manager in an aircraft factory. They're stepping up production, you know. The Führer has set new targets and said we have to be ready. It's Horst's job to make sure we meet them. It's so exciting. Such an honour, too!"

"Congratulations," said Harry, smiling his most synthetically charming smile at the young woman who was beaming with pride, "how nice." Harry hoped that the sarcasm of his comment would be wasted on the young couple. It was. They both returned his smile.

"How kind of you," commented Horst.

At Eger there was a delay. The town on the border between Bohemia and Lower Bavaria had long been a centre of Sudeten agitation. Harry had had a good friend there from his student days in Vienna. He had been invited to stay with Karl and his family several years previously. They had been hospitable and pleased that Karl had made new friends. Support for Konrad Henlein and the Sudeten German Party had been particularly ardent throughout the whole area. Harry's friendship with Karl had come to an abrupt end following a bruising argument about what Karl had called the re-awakening of Germany and his hope that one day Eger would become part of the new Reich which the Führer was building. He longed for the day they could welcome the Führer to Eger. As political tensions had increased, armed clashes had taken place between Czechs and Germans. Martial law had finally been declared by the embattled Czech authorities. What was Karl doing now, Harry wondered? Had he too donned the Nazi armband? Was he also one of those strutting their Aryan manhood around town? He hoped not but suspected that might be exactly what Karl was doing. He had no wish to have his curiosity satisfied.

"Prepare all travel documents for immediate inspection!" boomed a military sounding voice from somewhere along the corridor outside the compartment. Two men appeared, one in a black uniform, the other in civilian clothes. The six occupants of the compartment passed their papers to the two men who had slid open the compartment door. The check took only a few moments before the documents were returned. Not a single word had been exchanged. Harry breathed a sigh of relief and carefully replaced his papers in his briefcase, once again noticing the sandwiches which remained untouched. No, not yet; he could wait until they resumed their journey before biting into some of Mrs Fischlová's precious provisions.

This was the moment on the journey he had long dreaded. Although it was now six months since parts of his country had been swallowed wholesale by the Reich, he was finally leaving the territory of his former homeland and crossing into Germany proper. So much of what had happened in the preceding years now crowded into his fearful mind: the boycott, the anti-Jewish laws, the book burnings, the rallies at Nuremberg, the race laws, the hateful caricatures in *Der Stürmer*, the pogroms, the reports in the *Prager Tagblatt* of concentration camps from where former prisoners had been released with the intention of ensuring that tales of terror were spread amongst the population. He clasped his hands together tightly in a vain attempt to stop himself from trembling, his body tensed. The temptation to calm his nerves with a cigarette did not seem quite suited for the moment. He had grown accustomed to this small comfort when he felt anxious but now was not the time. He would stick it out a bit longer before stepping into the corridor once the train was rolling through the Bavarian countryside.

• • •

A few moments later, the door was again opened, this time by two different men in plain clothes.

"Walter Jentsch?" one of them enquired, looking directly at the elderly man, sitting pale and impassive in his seat. "Are you Walter Jentsch?"

"I am," replied the man.

"Take your baggage and come with us!"

The elderly man stood up, removed his single case from the rack above where he had been sitting and stepped out into the corridor.

"*Heil Hitler!*" said the other man standing by the door, who had not spoken so far. "Have a pleasant onward journey!".

"*Heil Hitler!*" snapped Horst and his wife in unison.

• • •

Silence descended on the five remaining passengers. From his seat by the window Harry could see Walter Jentsch being escorted along the platform towards a small group of men and women who had also been removed from the train.

Instinctively, Harry sought the comfort of his cigarette case. He offered his cigarettes to his travelling companions but Horst immediately declined.

"The Führer disapproves of tobacco, you know," the young woman explained, before adding that she and her husband had no objection to Harry smoking.

Silence returned. Harry stepped into the corridor where several men were also standing, cigarette in hand, breathing in the cold air through the open window as they exchanged desultory conversation.

"It was such an honour," a wiry young man was telling his neighbour, "greeting the Führer at the Party Rally."

"Yes, it must have been," had come the reply, "You must have felt so proud. I wish I could have been there!"

He resumed his seat and took refuge in a feigned sleep, surrendering to the gentle regular rocking motion of the train. As he dozed, his thoughts wandered. Here he was, travelling west towards the Rhine, the Dutch border and safety. But what of Arthur? Where was he at this moment? On a train, travelling east towards the Black Sea and the prospect of a boat ultimately to a safe haven? On a barge somewhere on the Danube, dodging the attention of hostile officials or maybe still stuck in Timisoara?

"I could have tried harder," Harry ruminated, "after all, I am the older brother." Regret mingled with a vague sense of guilt which Harry sensed but did not fully understand.

•••

The train progressed slowly through the gentle Bavarian countryside past Schirnding, Marktredwitz and Lauf an der Pegnitz. It was late when they finally pulled into Nuremberg.

Horst and his wife were quick to depart, cursorily bidding their fellow travellers farewell with another *"Heil Hitler"* to which the remaining three passengers did not reply. For over three hours since the enforced departure of Mr Jentsch they had all sat in stony silence. No-one had an appetite for small talk; Horst and his wife had been swift and enthusiastic with their Hitler greeting, a warning sign to their three fellow passengers.

•••

A platform announcement informed the passengers that the journey would be resumed early the following morning; passengers were welcome to make themselves comfortable on the train; the station buffet would remain open for light refreshments until midnight. By way of explanation, the announcer said that at night freight trains had priority. Harry was grateful for Mrs Fischlová's sandwiches. The other couple too had some provisions with them.

Germany, Wednesday 29 March 1939
Dawn was breaking as the train jolted into motion. No-one had joined the three passengers in the compartment. Harry suspected that his travelling companions might also be leaving Germany but caution prevailed and he decided against trying to satisfy his curiosity. A false move, an awkward explanation, anything in fact, could arouse suspicion. His fellow passengers might well be thinking the same and be equally disinclined to explore or reveal the purpose of their journeys. Yes, they were also bound for Hook of Holland but it would be foolish to conclude anything from the tiny scrap of information they had shared many hours ago. And so they sat facing each other, occasionally exchanging smiles and glances or anodyne comments about how pretty the Main Valley looked that spring day or how dramatic Würzburg appeared, as the train made its way along a particularly picturesque stretch of track by the river's edge.

Harry battled with the contradiction between these peaceful German landscapes, idyllic scenes of pastoral tranquility and beautiful historic towns and the knowledge that this same Germany was preparing for war, had already conquered its neighbour, his now former homeland and had instigated brutality and persecution in its concentration camps.

The train passed through Frankfurt. This, Harry told himself, recalling the lessons of his schooldays, was the birthplace of Johann

Wolfgang von Goethe, the epitome of the highest, most noble of German values. The contradiction with modern Germany was overwhelming. He could not reconcile the two. He was fleeing for his life from a Germany which presented him with a mortal threat and yet it was the words of Goethe and Schiller which came to mind. What, he asked himself, has Germany become.

The station, he observed from his corner seat, was bedecked with the symbol of the dictator and his party. Everywhere he looked, the red banners and the black twisted cross screamed at him.

German was his mother tongue; he had been schooled in German and studied for three years in Vienna, one of the great bastions of German culture. German had been the language he had shared with a number of girlfriends and more serious romantic attachments over the years. He had been steeped in a culture, a language and a world from which he was now escaping.

He had learned Italian, loved the language, the food, everything about the country apart from its preposterous strutting *duce*. He had embraced Paris with joy, had adored strolling free and unencumbered through the streets of the Latin Quarter; he had revelled in the night life, the food, the theatres, the art and the tiny attic room he had rented above a chaotic bookshop in the rue Cujas. In a relatively short space of time, he had developed fluency in the language which made him feel at home in the City of Light. He had also mastered sufficient English to be able to conduct business negotiations in that language, read newspapers, above all the *Manchester Guardian*; he had listened to talks on the BBC and enjoyed Dickens, Galsworthy and other novelists, even though he had never set foot in the country. He had planned to learn Spanish, which might be useful for business. Yet, despite all this, he, a supposed man of the world, was at heart a

German, or an Austrian German or a Bohemian German or a Jewish Bohemian Austro-German.

∴

As they sped towards Cologne, where he would have to change trains, all was confusion. The decision to flee had been rationally weighed and discussed with his parents, the fear they all felt, the dread that they too might fall victim to the rising terror of the Nazi regime, all that was real. Even if he did make it across the border and then on to England, his future was uncertain. He was adrift in a world unhinged, gone totally mad, irrational and dangerous.

Harry had been to Cologne only once before, ten years previously, when he had travelled to Paris. He had fond memories of his visit. It had been his first major foreign adventure away from home. He recalled vividly the combination of emotions, excitement, thrill, and at the same time faint trepidation. He had thrilled at pushing at the very boundaries of his experience. How little of the youthful exhilaration remained.

On that first journey in the autumn of 1929, he had also changed trains in Cologne where there was a five hour wait for the connection to Paris. Leaving his substantial baggage in the left-luggage office he had made his way out of the station towards the massive Gothic cathedral which towered high into the sky dominating everything. His original intention had been to wander into the Hohe Strasse and find something to eat. It would be a welcome change from the endless quantity of sandwiches with which his mother had equipped him and he particularly looked forward to his first taste of *Kölsch*, a beer unavailable in northern Bohemia. In the end he had strolled into the famous cathedral, just for a brief look and so that he could send his parents a postcard marking this stage of the journey. He had been entranced by its vastness, its spectacular glass windows, the acoustics and the view over the Rhine from the spire. He had climbed all 533 steps in the tower, proud of his achievement. When he glanced at his watch, he realised that he had spent so much time lost in awe that he needed to return promptly to the station. He would have to forgo his meal and his beer.

•••

"All passengers travelling onward to Hook of Holland must leave the train here," boomed the platform announcement as the train approached the platform. "Travellers in transit to Hook of Holland are strictly forbidden to leave the platform. This will be rigorously enforced. Prepare all documents for inspection! Remain on the platform! Any transgression will be severely punished!"

A few moments later, the announcement was repeated and as the train drew to a halt, a ticket inspector on the train appeared at the end of the corridor to ensure all passengers had received the instruction. If Harry had imagined he might grant himself a brief return visit to the cathedral, he now understood that absolute compliance with the announcement was essential. He was surprised by how many passengers remained on the platform. Many were struggling with heavy, bulky cases, carrying all their belongings with them, Harry assumed, or as much as they could manage. He caught sight fleetingly in his imagination of what he had left behind, in Reichenberg, in Trautenau, in Dvůr Králové and even in Prague. If ever he reached England, he would begin his new life there unencumbered by possessions. One day he would return and reclaim what belonged to him and his family. When might that be, he wondered.

Another rasping announcement informed them that there was no porter service on this platform; each traveller was responsible for their own luggage. Document inspection would begin shortly. Passengers should expect to open their cases. Every two or three paces along the platform stood an armed soldier surveying the scene. Harry looked around him. From the platform he could see clearly the mighty cathedral. Two huge swastika flags hung above its entrance porch as they did from the glass roof of the cavernous railway station.

The train that several hours later would take him to safety finally arrived. "Düsseldorf, Arnhem, Oldenzaal, Amsterdam and Hook of Holland" came another announcement. He climbed aboard and installed himself in the compartment designated by his reservation. The young couple with whom he had shared the journey from Prague were nowhere to be seen; they must have been seated elsewhere on the long train which was now filling up. Once again Harry would exercise caution and avoid getting drawn into conversations with strangers but he would treat himself to the last of his sandwiches. When that was gone, he would rely on the bar of chocolate which now constituted his iron rations. Perhaps it would taste even better once he had safely crossed the border. He would keep it as a reward, the first sweet taste of freedom.

•••

"All passengers must leave the train immediately. All passengers must ensure they have their luggage with them at all times. All documents must be ready for inspection."

The train had finally reached the border, after crawling along the Rhine making interminably slow progress. It had stood for ages in Duisburg and then again in Emmerich. The next station was Zevenaar not far from Arnhem and the safety of the Netherlands, beyond the reach of the Reich.

The German-Dutch border, Wednesday 29 to Thursday 30 March 1939

Slowly the train emptied its anxious cargo onto the platform. This was different from previous halts. Men in black uniforms, several with fierce-looking dogs held tightly on the leash, were stationed at regular intervals. The occasional bark had its intended intimidating effect. When all the cowed passengers had assembled, they were led away from the train and across a yard towards wooden structures where they were instructed to form queues. It was now getting dark and the evening air had a cold edge. It had been many hours since he had had something hot to eat or to drink. A cigarette would be comforting but he would wait until the formalities had been completed. To appear nonchalant at this moment might give a false impression; he felt anything but nonchalant. An air of intended menace hung heavy in the yard. Strange, he mused, how silent so many people can be. This was the final hurdle for those whose destination was anywhere but Germany. They had come so far, had suffered so much fear, hardship, loss and yet even now it could all go awry, here on the border, just as they approached the end of their ordeal. A collective understanding seemed to have spread through the crowd waiting now to travel into exile. Head down, mouth shut, eyes averted, complete compliance with the orders of the men in black.

They were divided into batches of five and ushered into a wooden hut. Across the floor stood a table behind which were seated several officials. In front of them was a book, a ledger perhaps, and an array of stamps, the bureaucrat's essential tools.

"Passports!" The five who had been summoned forward handed over their precious little booklets. Harry watched as the passports were laid out on the table in front of the officials who slowly scrutinised each document with infinite care, leafing through the pages. One of the passports, he noticed, was put to one side, the other four in a stack and slid to the left-hand side of the table. Was he the one or part of the four? Left or right? His papers were all in order but he could not be sure what this routine was supposed to signify other than a demonstration of their power and his powerlessness. Had a fault been spotted in one of his documents?

"Lewy," barked a voice, "forward, position one!" Position one, he assumed, was on the left where the four passports were stacked. He made his way to the table for the now familiar interrogation.

"Destination?"

"Hook of Holland."

"And then?"

"England."

"Empty your valuables on to the table: gold, diamonds, jewellery, Swiss watches, large denomination currency! Any attempt to conceal goods will be ruthlessly punished."

Harry slipped off his wristwatch and emptied the contents of his pockets. A few coins, a silver cigarette case and a lighter, a linen handkerchief.

"And the rest!"

"I'm sorry, that's it," replied Harry, almost amused by this distinctly unfunny pantomime. He did indeed have a valuable Swiss watch which he had been given as a barmitzvah present many years ago but he had left that with his parents in the expectation that he would be reunited with it sooner or later.

"We'll soon see," menaced the voice.

"Open your cases, Lewy!"

Harry once again did as instructed.

"List of contents!"

He presented the list he had shown in Prague when he had embarked on the journey.

"I ask you again: valuables: gold, diamonds, works of art, stamp collections, large denomination currency?"

"No, nothing of that kind," Harry repeated, as if following a script.

"Forbidden materials, enemy propaganda, books?"

"Just a few books with me," he answered, reaching into the smaller of his two cases.

"Take them out!"

"What's this? Zweig! Perverted Jewish rubbish!" said the official, grabbing hold of *Marie Antoinette* and flinging the book contemptuously onto a pile of other books in the corner which had previously escaped Harry's notice. He crammed the remaining books back into the case. Heine had survived, buried in the volume of selected German poetry. Zweig sacrificed for Heine. A good deal, Harry thought grimly.

He barely noticed as the official rummaged perfunctorily through both cases and rifled through the contents of the briefcase. The official continued:

"Shut your cases. Take off your shoes!"

The shoes also failed to reveal any hidden treasures.

"Take off your coat!"

Harry complied, removing the long shabby coat Mrs Fischlová had given him to reveal his elegant leather coat underneath.

"What's this? You didn't declare this, did you? Take it off! You've been warned. It's a serious crime to conceal property from the authorities of the Reich!"

Harry laid his leather coat on the table, instantly dismissing the idea of explaining that he had had no intention of concealing anything. He kept silent. There was no denying it looked expensive and stylish, its Italian cut distinguishing it from *ersatz* German versions.

"Very fine, indeed," said the interrogator, "would suit me well, don't you think, Lewy?"

He rose from his seat and took the coat, running his hand along the smooth leather back before slipping into it. It was immediately obvious that the coat was too small for him as he attempted to squeeze his fleshy body into it. It pinched under the arms and even as he tugged at the belt, he could not get it to close round him. Harry watched with alarm as the official flushed with anger and pulled it off, before hurling it back at its owner.

"Keep your damned coat, you filthy swine of a Jew!" he raged.

Harry remained silent. A stamp in his passport indicated that the procedures had been completed.

"Get lost, Jew!" said the official, pointing to the exit from the hut which led back to a platform where the train was waiting to take its passengers across to the Dutch side of the border.

•••

Harry climbed aboard, found an unreserved corner seat and waited. It took a long time for all the searches to be completed. He scarcely dared believe that the terrors of the previous six months were almost behind him and that he was on the threshold of a new life, that he might live again in freedom. Even at this late stage, something could still go wrong. Just be patient, he told himself, it won't be long now. He realised he was shivering, although it was not a cold night.

Those who had successfully navigated this final German checkpoint, from what he could see, the vast majority of his fellow passengers, gradually reboarded the train. At last, after many hours, a whistle on the platform signalled departure. The train began to move forward slowly towards the border.

The Netherlands, Thursday 30 March 1939
After a few miles, the train once again ground to a halt. It was long after midnight, too dark to see what was happening in the dimly lit station where they were standing. Then, with a hiss of steam and the clanking of metal couplings, it began to inch forwards again. At the end of the corridor a man in an unfamiliar uniform appeared and announced "Welcome to the Netherlands". For a split second, there was total silence and then deafening cheering broke out. Harry felt a wave of emotion rising within him, a huge release. He gave full throat to his relief.

"In a few moments we will be arriving in Zevenaar," the man continued, as the tumult gradually quietened down, "please have all your documents ready for inspection."

It was time, Harry decided, to reward himself. He reached into his briefcase for the bar of chocolate he had promised himself in celebration. It was missing. It had been there when the train had departed from Cologne and was still there as they had reached the final check on German soil.

•••

The formalities on the Dutch border were not particularly welcoming but neither were they heavy with the overt menace from which he had just escaped. The passengers, once again ordered to disembark from the train, were instructed to form two groups. Harry joined the second, smaller group. The first group comprised those whose destination was Amsterdam. Harry and his fellow passengers had all indicated their intention of travelling on to England. Once they had been given permission to travel through and under no circumstances remain in the Netherlands, they were told to take the train standing at the neighbouring platform. This would take them to Oldenzaal. They could expect further checks with representatives of a British organisation involved in the reception of refugees from Czechoslovakia. Harry glanced at the latest entry stamped into his passport: *Doorlaatpass*, permission to transit the Netherlands.

As dawn broke the train crawled through the flat, orderly countryside, stopping frequently. At Oldenzaal the train pulled into a siding. Once again the familiar routine followed. Ushered off the train by courteous but armed guards, the passengers entered a small waiting room where two desks had been set up, staffed by a man and a woman. From the style of their clothes Harry guessed they must be English. A short conversation in English ensued. Harry confirmed his intention in due course to travel on from England to the United States, where he had an uncle.

"Do you have a visa to enter the USA?" asked the woman.

"No, not yet, I have applied, but I do have an affidavit from the American Legation in Prague which says that is my destination. Would you like to see it?"

"Oh, I don't think that will be necessary at the moment," interjected the man, gesturing airily that Harry should proceed to the waiting train. Harry breathed a quiet sigh of relief. The expenditure incurred surreptitiously in Prague had, after all, been worthwhile.

The train seemed to dawdle but the journey no longer held the latent terror of every minute on German soil which had been his constant companion since his departure from Prague. However, there were now a few empty seats. Evidently not all those who had paraded in front of the English officials had been able to continue their travels. The approach to Hook of Holland was endlessly slow but entirely bearable. A ferry awaited him to transport him to Harwich. He already knew he would yet again have to have his documents ready for inspection and be prepared for another set of questions.

The evening crossing was rough and Harry decided he would not make a good sailor. He realised he had never spoken to his father about his voyage from Europe to Cape Town, albeit under very different circumstances. He would correct this omission, he vowed, once they were reunited, whenever that might be. For the time being he had to concentrate on what lay immediately ahead. On board Harry recognised the young couple with whom he had shared a compartment on the first stage of the journey from Prague.

"So you're going to England, too," the man said.

Harwich, England Friday 31 March 1939
Disembarkation and arrival at Harwich followed the pattern now familiar to Harry: long queues, officials at desks, lists, inspection of documents but this time without barked orders, men in black, screaming red, black and white flags, dogs, distressed or humiliated travellers. Just waiting and more waiting. Harry was pointed towards a table with a banner saying "Refugee Committee" but was too tired after his sleepless overnight crossing slumped on a couch to absorb much of the information directed at him. He received a sheet of typewritten instructions, glanced fleetingly at the heading "Important Advice for Refugees" and placed it carefully inside his briefcase. Later would do.

"Don't forget to register with the Refugee Committee when you get to Liverpool Street," he heard someone behind the desk tell him.

Harry gazed at the banner above the reception desk in the reception area. So, it's official now, he mused as he turned the word over slowly in his head as if examining a curious looking shell just washed up on a beach. "Ref-u-gee," that's what I am," now saying the word out loud in English to no-one in particular.

"You must be exhausted, darling," came a voice, "here, have a nice cuppa tea and a sandwich or two!"

He had not noticed a woman approach him as he sat resting for a moment at a table. She reminded him vaguely of Mrs Fischlová, about the same indeterminate age, a red patterned headscarf atop a worn, weary face.

"This'll perk you up no end, my love," she continued.

A large chipped blue and white striped steaming mug was pressed into his hand and a plate with a mound of white triangular slices of bread placed in front of him.

"Here you are, darling, cheese sandwiches, made them myself! Tuck in!"

"Thank you," Harry replied, carefully pronouncing a phrase he had practised and perfected, "how very kind of you." He had not given any thought to what arrival in England would actually be like. To that point England had been an almost abstract concept, a place of safety. He was unsure what he had been expecting but it was not this.

She smiled. He took a sip. It was hot, sickly sweet, unlike anything he had ever tasted before. It was not the coffee he yearned for but he would have to get used to it. The cheese in the sandwiches seemed to have a rubber-like consistency. An old German saying came to mind, *andere Länder, andere Sitten,* different countries, different customs. He was in England.

•••

The type-written sheet of instructions he had slipped into his briefcase contained an address in West London to which he was directed by the Refugee Committee. A Mrs Parker would provide him with a room. The instructions also informed him that an appointment had been made for him to attend for an interview at 10.00am prompt on 5 April at the offices of the British Committee for Refugees from Czechoslovakia. Punctual attendance was vital, stated the instructions and this was underlined in red for emphasis. Later, Mrs Parker told him the address was in an area called Bloomsbury, very close to the British Museum, more than an hour's walk at a brisk pace.

•••

"Come in, Mr Lewy, please take a seat!" A man in a checked suit indicated the chair in front of a desk which reminded Harry of his own long-abandoned imposing desk in Reichenberg.

"I am Major Reginald Hutton-Dacre and my colleague here is Mr Ladislav Ševčik. We represent the British Committee for Refugees from Czechoslovakia. We need to ask you a few questions and fill in this form here to get you officially registered with us."

"I see," said Harry.

"I expect you have heard of us," continued the Major, his booming voice filling the narrow office. Harry cast a glance around the Major's domain. The blue, white and red flag of Czechoslovakia, intertwined with a Union Jack, adorned the wall behind the desk, on a corner of which stood a bronze bust of TG Masaryk. On the wall to his right he noticed a portrait of former President Beneš and a photograph of Prague Castle. Every spare inch of shelf and cupboard space seemed to be piled high with manila-coloured folders, some bulging, others looking as if they contained a mere sheet or two. As if divining Harry's thoughts, the Major added:

"Yes, records of everyone from Czechoslovakia who finds themselves in this country at this unhappy time. Shall we make a start, Mr Lewy?"

Harry nodded his agreement; after all that was the purpose of the summons to appear in front of these two gentlemen.

"So, place and date of birth, please."

"Trautenau, 18th February 1909."

"Here we use the Czech not the German name," said Mr Ševčik, speaking for the first time. Harry observed as he wrote Trutnov on the form.

"And in Prague?"

"I didn't have an address in Prague, Harry replied cautiously. "I wasn't registered with the police. It was too dangerous."

"You must have lived somewhere," persisted Mr Ševčik.

"I rented a room," Harry continued, "in the 12th district, in Blanická." Mr Ševčik appeared satisfied and did not ask for further details. Harry was relieved. He had no reason to be wary but nonetheless instinct told him to avoid disclosing too much information about Mrs Fischlová. Harry felt uncomfortable; the interview, he thought, had not got off to the best of starts.

Now it was the Major's turn: "And the reason for leaving Czechoslovakia?"

"I couldn't remain there any longer. It wasn't safe for people like me." Harry paused. He decided it would be unwise to complain about the harsh measures introduced by the Czech government even before the Nazi occupation on 15th March. "As you can tell from my name, I am Jewish."

"Of course," commented the Major, "we classify the reason as 'racial'."

"The Home Office has given you permission to stay in England for a short while. Please may I have a look at the permit they have issued to you?"

Harry placed the document in Mr Ševčik's out-stretched hand.

"Until 4th July 1939," noted Mr Ševčik, "you can stay for three months. What are your plans after that? You know you can't stay here any longer than that?"

"I have an uncle in Paterson in New Jersey. I am hoping to travel to the United States."

"Perfect, we have very limited funds; it is our duty to ensure that while you are here you do not become a burden to the government, or as we say here, "the public purse". The English are a very generous people, you know, but they do not like paying for foreigners. I am sure you understand."

"Yes, I do," replied Harry. "I have never been a burden to any one and I will not start now."

"Good, as long as we understand each other, Mr Lewy", continued the Major, leafing through some papers. "That's what you told our people in Oldenzaal, so everything is in order. Splendid."

"Is that it?" asked Harry.

"Not quite, there are a few more matters we need to discuss," answered the Major curtly. "What political involvement did you have?"

"None," replied Harry, before adding hesitantly, "I did pay a subscription for a while to The Jewish Party, just a few crowns a year, nothing more."

"Did you hold elected office in the Jewish Party? Were you an activist? Distribute propaganda?" enquired Mr Ševčik, suddenly appearing to take a greater interest in the interview.

"No, not at all. I wasn't active. I sympathised with some of their ideas and their opposition to Henlein. That's all."

"Ah, yes, makes sense," said the Major, "after all, you are a 'racial'".

A short silence prevailed.

"And now the question of means. Tell us about your means, Mr Lewy."

"Means?" asked Harry, uncertainty about the question clear in his voice.

"Means, money, what money do you have to live on here in England?"

Harry stared blankly at both his interrogators but said nothing. He had anticipated that this issue would arise sooner or later. Outside he could see the magnificent pillars at the entrance to the British Museum. What untold riches would he discover there? Rain was falling from a leaden London sky.

He turned to reply to the Major.

"Means? Money? I have nothing," he answered barely audibly and avoided looking directly at the men sitting in front of the flags.

"So, nothing, in England. What about elsewhere, in France, in the USA?"

"Nothing," repeated Harry.

"In Czechoslovakia?"

"The Nazis seized my bank account. There were about 15,000 Czech crowns in it at the time, last October. I was allowed to take 10 Reichsmarks out of the country when I left. That's it."

"Valuables?"

The question now irritated Harry. He had heard it too frequently in the course of the preceding weeks as he had passed from one check or control to another.

"One silver cigarette case, the clothes I am wearing, a spare pair of shoes, two shirts, a few books and this wrist-watch." He paused. "No gold coins, jewels or precious stones." Harry paused again. "And no works of art."

The Major scribbled a note on the questionnaire on the desk in front of him.

"And one final question," continued the Major, " do you have any relatives or friends here who can assist you financially?"

"No, apart from a distant relative of my mother who lives in Scotland. I don't know him or anything about him but I can write and ask if he can help. He's called Mr Falk."

Harry looked down at his once elegant shoes.

"I can always see if Mr Falk can help."

"That would be a good idea. Do that!" said Mr Ševčik.

There was nothing more Harry could say.

"I apologise for asking such questions," the Major continued, "they are purely routine. I am sure you understand, we are only doing our job."

Harry attempted a vague smile.

"What the Committee can do is provide you with some small financial support." This time it was Mr Ševčik who was speaking. "You will need to report here each week. We will take care of the rent at Edith Road and grant you a regular sum of One Pound and five Shillings. You will have to meet all expenses from that amount. There can be no additional payments. You will have to manage very carefully. No extravagance. No high living. I am sure you understand."

"Yes," Harry confirmed," I am very grateful", before adding, "I am not used to living on charity."

"Of course not," boomed the Major as he stood up and escorted Harry to the door. "We'll see you next week."

•••

Weeks later, sitting in his cold damp room in a three-storey house in Edith Road, Harry reflected. The journey which had taken him half way across Europe, from Prague to Oldenzaal and ultimately on to London had at the time been an ordeal, days and nights with fear a constant companion and with no guarantee that he would ever reach his destination. The bedroom in which he now lived had an unwelcome familiarity to it: a narrow bed, a small dressing table, a wardrobe and a rickety desk. A worn rug partially covered the floorboards. The single light bulb gave out a feeble, inadequate light. A small window through which the sunlight rarely penetrated looked out over a shabby yard, contributing to a general gloom which well matched his state of mind. In essence it was the latest version of the rooms he had inhabited ever since the night he had fled from Reichenberg. Dvůr Králové, Prague, London all offered similar minimal comforts to a single man without means or a permanent roof over his head.

Harry resisted the temptation to sink into self-pity but could not help remembering wistfully the elegant comfort of his smart bachelor flat in Reichenberg with its solid respectable desk and bookcases lovingly crafted to his specification by Alois and filled with an eclectic mixture of books, postcards and framed photographs. Who, he wondered, was living there now? No doubt the flat had been confiscated, 'aryanised', and let to a suitable tenant, the previous occupant suddenly having disappeared. Who might be the beneficiary? Was it a local opportunist, someone Harry might even have known, a former classmate from Trautenau perhaps, now moving up in the world, was it an official of the Reich from across the border? All he knew was that he had been able to call it his home. He had never given much thought to the matter until events had forced him into this perilous twilight world. He had acquired a new occupation; he was now a professional refugee.

"Well. I didn't need years of study for this, did I, or much training either? Turns out I had all the qualifications that mattered," he muttered to himself with grim ironic satisfaction. "Passed every examination, *cum laude*, with honours, to become a beggar."

However lonely and miserable he felt now as he came to terms with the unending reality of being a refugee, it felt like a genuine achievement to have got away. He had survived the perils of growing Czech repression and then crossing Nazi Germany. In truth the journey had been relatively uneventful; he had avoided anything worse than routine harassment and low-level abuse, unpleasant but also not surprising; he had not come to the attention of the Nazi authorities apart from the incident of the coat on the border. It was not a journey he would wish to undertake again; he hoped that when the time came for his parents to make their way to England, their British passports would hold good and protect them from any excesses.

In a letter to his father and mother, still in Dvůr Králové, he played down the fear he had known and chose instead to say how peaceful and beautiful the German countryside looked from the train. Was he perhaps exaggerating and giving the impression of simply going on a holiday? He had written similar anodyne letters from Florence. He was more guarded about his feelings and circumstances now that he was in London. He did not want to alarm them. He described the beauty of London's parks, the splendour of its great museums and galleries, the majesty of the river flowing through the heart of the imperial city. It felt as if he was composing a travelogue. Would they be sceptical or just be pleased to hear from him? He avoided reference to the very visible preparations for war, the gnawing anxiety about Arthur and the small privations, the reality of daily life as a down-at-heel, almost destitute, refugee.

5.
ALIEN

London, Spring 1939

Harry found the English puzzling.

Lying on his narrow bed, musing about how he should spend the day, he remembered a booklet buried at the bottom of his briefcase and retrieved it.

When he had registered with the Refugee Committee at Liverpool Street, someone had pressed the small blue booklet into his hand. He had not paid any attention at the time and now was not sure who had given it to him, an official of some sort.

He studied it intently. *While you are in England: helpful information and guidance for every refugee.* It looked official. Closer scrutiny revealed it had been produced by the German Jewish Aid Committee and the Jewish Board of Deputies. It was written in English with a German version on each facing page. The helpful information and guidance consisted of a series of formal instructions expressed in stern forbidding language. The German text called them *Ehrenpflichten*, obligations of honour. He started reading carefully.

Instruction One was common sense, he thought. He was already using every opportunity to learn English and speak it intelligibly. He did not regard this as an obligation. He relished learning languages. The circumstances made it urgent but he needed no encouragement.

The second instruction he also found obvious, namely to avoid speaking German in public places, but he was amused by the injunction, stated in italics, *do not talk in a loud voice.* Is this what we do, we refugees and foreigners, Harry wondered. He understood the preference for *halting English rather than fluent German* but accepted the best he might achieve was heavily accented fluency and nobody would be fooled by that.

It was the third and fourth instructions which grabbed his attention. *Do not criticise any Government regulations or the way things are done over here....do not join any Political organisation or take part in any political activities.* Harry noted the capital P. He had never considered himself to be "political". He had no intention of becoming an agitator but England was the land of liberty and free speech. Would he need to be more careful than he had imagined? It was probably sound advice but something jarred vaguely in these instructions. Did they really mean he should avoid having opinions at all or just that, as a foreigner only temporarily in the country, he was expected or even required to keep them to himself?

The fifth instruction confirmed the view taking shape in his mind that living in England would undoubtedly be a complicated business. Here, he felt as he read the words aloud, first in English, then in German and once again in English, was the real challenge: *Do not make yourself conspicuous by speaking loudly, nor by your manner or dress. The Englishman greatly dislikes ostentation, loudness of dress or manner, or unconventionality of dress or manner. The Englishman attaches very great importance to modesty, understatement in speech rather than overstatement and quietness of dress and manner. He values good manners....*

So much attention to appearances, he said to himself.

On balance, Harry thought, he could comply without too much difficulty with these requirements though it would take time to acquire the gift of under-statement. He flicked through the remainder of the booklet in desultory fashion. The message was keep your head down, your mouth shut and stay as much out of sight as possible. Fleetingly he recalled the advice Heinz had given him on his arrival in Prague a few fraught weeks previously as he prepared to enter his twilight existence. That had been very different. Here, in London, he might be isolated in unfamiliar surroundings but he was not in immediate danger. For that he should be grateful, as the little blue booklet repeatedly reminded its reader. Gratitude was important.

He was still not sure what to make of the English, despite this well-meaning advice.

One moment, he would encounter a cold indifference, verging on rudeness or even haughtiness, the next, a warm friendliness verging on the intimate and willingness to help in whatever way possible. He could never be sure. Perhaps, he speculated, it was the ever-changing weather, the one topic of conversation which it was safe and uncontroversial for him to engage in, which shaped the English character.

•••

As a recently arrived single man, he was required to report regularly to the authorities. He had been in London for less than a week when he went to report for the first time to the police. It was a damp miserable day with a swirling cold east wind as Harry climbed the red sandstone steps to the local police station. A sign indicated the Aliens

Department. He walked into a waiting room, removing his hat as he entered. The two rows of wooden seats were empty. He sat down at the end of the front row. Good, no queue, I won't have to wait for hours. From behind a frosted glass panel, he could hear raised voices but he could not make out what was being said. Suddenly a door opened and a dishevelled figure in a shabby brown raincoat emerged, head down, scuttling towards the exit, followed by a man in a dark suit.

"And don't come back until you have got your papers in order!" bellowed the dark suit, turning on his heels and disappearing again into his office.

Harry was trembling slightly; he could not completely overcome the unease which took hold of him every time he had to deal with officialdom. He fingered the cigarette case in his jacket pocket.

"Next!" came an instruction from the office door which had been flung open by the man in the suit. He was smallish, of slight build and sporting a thin moustache. Perhaps, a former soldier Harry speculated as he entered the office. The official had resumed his seat behind the desk in front of which Harry now stood, holding his briefcase in one hand, his hat in the other.

"Name!" said the official, curtly, without glancing up at the man standing in front of him.

"Lewy, Leon Harry Lewy."

"Papers, please". Harry noted the 'please'. An improvement. He handed over his documents for scrutiny. The official stretched out towards the stand on his desk on which were mounted a number of stamps. Carefully he selected the relevant seal of authority but then he paused, holding the stamp in mid-air.

"You're a German, Mr Lewy, is that correct?"

"No sir, I am not a German."

"But it says here your place of birth is..." he stumbled over the pronunciation, "...is Trow-ten-ow, in the German Reich."

"Yes, it is, Trautenau, in Czechoslovakia, or at least it was in Czechoslovakia, until...." Harry left the sentence incomplete. He shifted his weight from foot to foot, standing awkwardly in front of the desk. The usual 'please take a seat' had on this occasion not been forthcoming and the chair next to where he was standing remained unoccupied.

"So, you're Czech then? Except that Czechoslovakia no longer exists, does it?"

"That's correct."

"But you speak German, if I'm not mistaken, which in my book makes you German, if I get the drift."

Was the official being deliberately obtuse, Harry wondered, intentionally making him feel uncomfortable, belittling him.

"We have to be very careful these days, you know what I mean?" continued the official, as if sensing Harry's discomfort and being happy to extend it for a few moments longer. "So, you are stateless but German," he concluded.

"German is my mother tongue, but I am not a German and yes, I have a Czech passport but I am effectively stateless," Harry explained again, struggling to remain patient, knowing that any show of irritation or temper would only exacerbate and prolong the interview. The official still would not relent.

"Any other languages, then, or nationalities or countries you would care to mention?" He looked up at Harry, peering intently at him. Harry noticed the official's tone.

"I speak Italian and French, Czech, some Spanish and I am learning English."

"How very cosmopolitan," commented the official, "and Hebrew?"

"Hebrew?" replied Harry incredulously.

"Yes, do you speak Hebrew?"

"No, not Hebrew."

"Just curious," came the explanation, "it's just that so many of you fellows who breeze in here these days expecting us to help, seem to be Hebrews. You know what I mean?"

Harry understood fully but chose to say nothing, instead smiling wanly.

The stamp thudded emphatically onto the document lying on the desk.

"That's all for now, Mr Lewy, you may go. Thank you for coming to see us. Please report again in a fortnight's time."

Harry nodded, turned and left. Outside the police station the damp April air now felt refreshing.

He had set about improving his English as rapidly as possible and was proud of his progress, thanks to the little wireless which his landlady, Mrs Parker, had obtained for him from the nearby second-hand shop. Shortly after he had moved in, she had asked him if there was anything he needed. For years Harry had read at least one daily newspaper and in better times he had listened avidly to the wireless, following news bulletins with particular attention. He had asked shyly if there was any possibility that she might find a small wireless set and he had been delighted when a few days later, she presented him with one. It adorned his sparsely furnished room. Harry was desperate for news on which he could rely. He had always prided himself on being well informed. Rumour abounded and fed his anxiety.

The wireless was a godsend. He spent hours night and day listening to the BBC National Programme. The voices were so impeccably clear and easy to follow. In particular he listened assiduously to the Weather Forecast which equipped him admirably to engage in daily conversations with Mrs Parker. He wondered if she had ever been to Cumberland, Westmoreland, Northumberland and Durham but limited his exchanges with her to observations about how changeable the weather was, with showers and sunny intervals and cloudy patches. Mrs Parker was perfectly satisfied. The news bulletins, on the other hand, were unsettling. The drift towards war was inexorable.

Mrs Parker was garrulous; in other circumstances Harry might have found her endless chatter tiresome but he was grateful for her spontaneous streams of consciousness. Hers was certainly not the cultured voice of the BBC but she was cheerful, lively and occasionally very funny. She was, she had explained to him, a real Cockney, although she had moved 'up west'.

•••

"What you up to today then?" she enquired cheerily one morning. as he made his way into the hall.

Harry was non-committal, not yet familiar with this kind of English small-talk.

"I am not very busy," he replied rather formally, adding " but I do have an appointment later on this afternoon."

"Lovely day for a walk," she continued. Harry feigned polite interest. "It's really pretty down by the river, Hammersmith way, not far from here. Do you know where I mean?"

"Not exactly," Harry answered courteously.

"Well," she said, guiding him towards the door, "you go left here, down the bottom of the road, turn left, past The Nelson, keep going and you can't miss it."

"That is very kind of you, Mrs Parker."

"No trouble at all, Dr Lewy, you just say if you want anything! All right?"

"I will," he replied. "London is so big I will need time to get to know it."

• • •

Harry was pleased with these little exchanges with his landlady. He may be doing nothing more than passing the time of day but with each conversation he felt his confidence growing. She had told him he was doing well and did not sound all that foreign at all. Most difficult were the short spontaneous casual exchanges, so different from the formal class-room business language he had been taught. He would make progress, he was sure.

Mrs Parker knew London intimately and was a mine of essential advice, about bus routes, opening times, the latest regulations, where to get a good cheap hot meal, where to keep warm, the location of the best museums. Harry was grateful for this last piece of information. He had time on his hands and in the coming months would spend hours in the British Museum and The National Gallery. Anywhere where he did not have to use a few pennies of the meagre allowance he received from the refugee charity.

"If you need anything, Dr Lewy, just ask," ran her morning mantra as she poured him a cup of weak tea. In truth, he needed a cup of strong coffee, but tact dictated that he should thank her enthusiastically for the steaming hot beverage which began each day. Twice a week, which was all he could afford, he would fortify himself with an espresso from a little café run by Italian exiles which he had spotted near the tube station. He could even practise his Italian, which delighted Marco and Paolo enormously. Harry was equally pleased. They called him *dottore*.

•••

Would his parents be interested in any of this? Possibly.

They would more likely be pleased to know that he had been invited to a Passover *Seder* by a complete stranger just after he had arrived. As he was registering with the refugee reception committee set up on the concourse of Liverpool Street Station he had fallen into conversation with a man of about his own age whose duty appeared to be to welcome the new arrivals before they began to tackle the paper-work.

"Hello," the stranger had said, approaching Harry. "You look a bit lost. Where have you come from?"

Harry was taken aback. He had not expected yet another interrogation although this impromptu questioning sounded friendly and in no way threatening. Without thinking, Harry replied: "Hook of Holland."

"No, no, I mean before that! Where do you really come from?"

Harry paused before replying, turning over the various possibilities in his mind. This was in reality a much more complicated question than it might have appeared to the stranger. Finally he said carefully: "I have come from the Sudetenland via Prague."

"Jewish?" queried the stranger.

"Yes, Jewish," Harry said softly, injecting a note of caution into the exchange.

The stranger had immediately sensed the slight shift in tone.

"No need to worry, we're all Jews round here," he said, casting a glance at the groups of people assembled in the makeshift reception centre.

Harry nodded.

"It's *Pesach* in a few days from now. I don't suppose you have anywhere to go to celebrate the Passover?"

"No, I don't suppose I have," he replied, "I haven't given it a second thought. I have had other things to think about."

"Of course you have. Well, then, you must come to us. We don't live far from here, we haven't got much but you're very welcome to share what we have. It would be an honour," said the man in a tone which brooked no refusal.

"Meyer Rosenberg," he said, stretching out his hand in greeting, "very pleased to meet you. Welcome to London!".

"Harry Lewy," came the rejoinder, "pleased to meet you."

And so, in April 1939, shortly after arriving in London, Harry had found himself guest of honour around a small but heavily laden table in a terraced house somewhere in Whitechapel in London's East End. The Rosenberg family had assembled. Harry marvelled at how many people could cram into such a tiny space. The dining room obviously also doubled on normal days as the main living space. A pile of books, magazines and leaflets had been stacked untidily in a corner out of the way of the *Seder* guests.

Mr Rosenberg presided. Prayers and blessings were said. The customary Passover dishes, the hard-boiled egg in salt water, the bitter herbs, the sweet *charoset*, the unleavened *matzos* bread, reminded Harry how familiar proceedings had once been. The ancient Passover story of hope and salvation was recounted. Harry did not need to be reminded of why this was a special night but Mr Rosenberg stressed to the assembled company that it was a special privilege for them to be able to include their guest as part of their celebration. It was a very long time since Harry had drunk a glass of wine, let alone the four glasses which formed an integral part of the ceremony. He could barely recall the last time he had taken part in any kind of celebration.

"Tonight," Mr Rosenberg intoned, "we remember our deliverance from slavery in Egypt; we remember how the Angel of God protected the People of Israel and how Moses led us to safety and freedom." Harry was lost in thought when Mr Rosenberg turned towards him.

"And would our dear guest, recently delivered from the torments of Germany, like to say a few words?"

Harry was caught unprepared.

"I would like to say thank you for your kindness." Everyone applauded. "I would also like us to say a prayer for my father, Max, my mother Minna, and my brother, Arthur. They are far away and in danger. May they be with us next year!"

The high-spirited joviality around the table subsided as Mr Rosenberg rose to his feet.

"And may we hope that next year the family of our guest will be with us here in London. It would be an honour."

"Amen," responded the tiny congregation in the makeshift dining room.

The moment of solemnity passed and conversation resumed. It turned out Mr Rosenberg was the son of immigrants from near Memel on the Baltic. They had made their way to England nearly fifty years previously to escape the threat of conscription into the Russian army and the pogroms which raged at the time. He was a 'proper Londoner' now, he said and proud of it, even if many people did not welcome Jews in their midst. Here they were safe, he told Harry. They had kept the Blackshirts out of their streets only a few years ago. They would not hesitate to do it again. He worked in a textile factory, a bit of a sweat-shop really but it paid the rent, as he put it. And was a socialist, like all of his friends. Was Harry perhaps interested, was he a member of a party or a union?

•••

The dreary routine of registering with the authorities no longer held any terrors for Harry. Officialdom, he thought, was much the same the world over. Here at least no-one shouted or tried to intimidate you, apart from the very occasional self-important official one could find everywhere. The slightly unpleasant first encounter at the police station stood out in his mind as the exception rather than the rule but it was nonetheless a warning that he could never truly relax. A dull civility seemed the order of the day. Life consisted of endless queuing; another stamp on another document, another questionnaire to complete, one more visibly bored official taking an age to scrutinise the answers before landing his stamp with a noisy flourish on the bottom of each page. Those in uniform were generally courteous and yes, it was acceptable to ask a policeman in the street for directions. Gone was the constant dread which had corroded his nerves. He might be officially regarded as an alien but for the moment this entailed no greater obligation or threat than a regular appearance at the local police station in West Kensington, the 'nick' as Mrs Parker called it. He could cope with that. The regular visits to the Refugee Committee provided him with enough to eke out a careful existence. One can even get used to being a beggar, he thought.

•••

His thoughts turned constantly to his parents. He wrote regularly. The first letter was the hardest. One evening shortly after his arrival as daylight was fading, he had sat at the small desk in his room, staring for ages at the sheet of paper in front of him, his fountain pen poised but immobile, unsure what to include and what to omit.

I'll make it short, he had resolved, enough to let them know I am safe and well. And so a painstaking final draft of carefully crafted blandness emerged.

> "Dear father, dear mother,
>
> I arrived safely a few days ago and have found lodgings. They are satisfactory but London is much bigger than I had ever imagined. I am walking more than I ever used to. My landlady is called Mrs P. She is kind and chats a lot. We talk about the weather which is good for my English. Everyone here talks about the weather, just like in the books. The parks in London are also beautiful. You will like them.
>
> I will tell you all the details of my journey when you arrive but in the meantime I hope your preparations are going well. Please do not leave it too late. Come as soon as you can get your papers in order! People here say war is coming.
>
> Do you have any news of Arthur? If you are in contact, please give him my address. I will do what I can to help him get a visa. I am going to do the same for W. but I have no idea how to find so much money. £100.00 is a fortune!
>
> I will close now. I miss you very much and think of you constantly but you do not need to worry about me. I have everything I need. I will write to Belfast soon.
>
> Your loving son

•••

His first visit to the local post office had left him disconcerted.

"Where to?" snapped the young post-mistress in response to Harry's request for a postage stamp.

"To Czechoslovakia, please," he had replied automatically.

"Doesn't exist anymore," had come the answer. "Do you mean Germany or the Protectorate of Bohemia and Moravia?"

Harry had hesitated for a moment, unsure, before confirming that the letter was destined for the Protectorate. As he affixed the small orange 2d stamp with the head of King George VI on it, the voice behind the counter said:

"Well, I don't suppose it matters, does it, it's all the same really?"

"I don't suppose it does," Harry replied, thinking the opposite.

The encounter reminded him of how far away his parents were, out of reach but not out of harm's way. When would he hear from them in reply? He felt thoroughly dejected.

•••

Harry had never walked so far and so frequently. With time on his hands and very little money in his pockets, he took to spending hours in public libraries and museums which were free, warm and stocked with intellectual nourishment. Once a week on a Saturday he would allow himself the luxury of buying the *Manchester Guardian*. He thought of Max, a devoted reader following a business trip to Belfast in the 1920s. Harry would then pore over every article for the best part of the following week, filling empty hours in this manner. What have I achieved today, he would ask himself, imagining the blank expression on his face in answer.

Along with other refugees he would visit the Lyons Corner House on Tottenham Court Road. It had become a kind of informal community centre for the displaced of Europe, he thought, useful in its own way but not the kind of place he would normally seek out for enjoyment but a cup of tea or coffee was in the reach of the most impoverished outcasts.

The majority assembled there were Jewish refugees from Germany, Austria, Czechoslovakia and occasionally Budapest, mainly single men or men now through circumstance on their own who had lived generally assimilated lives in the countries they regarded as home. Some were former soldiers who had fought in the uniform of the Austrian or German armies and now struggled to abandon their loyalty to the countries which had so harshly abandoned them.

He observed how they reflected the distinctive characteristics of their erstwhile homelands, the diverse local traditions and distinctive identities which had developed across centuries in the patchwork of central and western Europe. To the outside world, however, and to the British authorities they were all much the same: Jews, refugees and foreigners, aliens to be viewed with caution if not downright suspicion or at worst, even hostility. One thing was sure: Harry was not unique as he surveyed the patrons of this unusual coffee house.

All had stories to tell, not dissimilar from his own. For those whose more orthodox practice of Judaism involved regular attendance at synagogue, Lyons Corner House performed a more limited function, but for those like Harry, for whom attendance at *shul* had long since ceased to be a part of their lives, this unstylish coffee house provided an opportunity for occasional company. It was also a source of invaluable information and gossip, as well as less than helpful rumours. From time to time former acquaintances from the past would recognise each other and nod respectfully in acknowledgement of their shared fate. News would travel fast about who was now in London and who was still trying to get to safety.

One day a waitress approached Harry as he sat at a table, slowly sipping a hot milky liquid which passed as coffee.

"Dr Lewy?" she enquired cautiously. She was holding a photograph of a younger Harry in her right hand, along with an envelope.

"Yes," he replied, "that's me."

"I have a message for you," she said, passing him the envelope.

Intrigued, Harry took the envelope, instantly recognising the handwriting. It was from Trudie, who, it turned out, had also made her way to London and was working as a live-in maid for a wealthy family in Belsize Park. She had heard that he was in London, the note inside explained. She would be so pleased to see him again, gave her current address and suggested a date and time. He should come to the rear of the mansion and knock three times on the kitchen door. Harry was amused at the pretence of an assignation. How very Trudie, he sighed.

•••

On the appointed date Harry set out from West Kensington. It would take a little over an hour to walk through Hyde Park to Paddington. As the weather was fine, he would find a bench in the park and read for a while and then take the bus. Mrs Parker had stopped him briefly that morning on his way out.

"Morning, Dr Lewy," she had said breezily, handing him a book, "You might like this; a friend lent it me. Let me have it back when you're done, no hurry!"

"Thank you, Harry replied, "Very kind of you."

•••

At Paddington he found the bus-stop where a double-decker was already filling up with passengers. He made his way to the upper deck, finding a seat next to the window. A middle-aged man sat down next to him.

"Going far?" the man asked.

"Belsize Park," replied Harry.

"Mind if I ask where you come from?" asked the man who had noticed Harry's accent even in the two words he had uttered. Harry hesitated. How much explanation should he give or would Protectorate suffice? He loathed the Nazi terminology imposed on his country.

"Czechoslovakia," he answered, conscious at that moment of sounding German. He took a cigarette out of the treasured silver case and lighting up, offered one to his neighbour. The man declined.

"I see," continued the man. Harry had grown used to these kinds of conversations, which usually ended with a non-committal, "Oh, I see." On this occasion the conversation took a different direction.

"I am so terribly sorry, what our government did was a betrayal. The Munich so-called agreement is a shameful document." Harry was taken aback. Political discussions did not take place on the upper deck of London buses. "We are all paying the price, now," continued the stranger, enquiring "do you personally know the Sudetenland?"

"Yes, that's where I come from," Harry replied, not wanting to prolong the conversation, "but I'm a refugee now."

"Oh, I see," came the answer, as expected.

The journey to Belsize Park did not take long. Harry got to his feet.

"Excuse me, please," he said as he stepped into the aisle.

"I am sorry, very very sorry about all that has happened to your country," answered the man as he pressed a crumpled piece of paper into Harry's hand.

Carefully manoeuvring himself down the stairs as the bus drew to a halt, Harry glanced at the paper in his hand. It was a ten-shilling note. A fortune. Harry was utterly bewildered.

By the time he knocked on the kitchen door he was in high spirits. He and Trudie had once been very close. He had liked the

Berger household in Vienna where her parents had always warmly welcomed him; they and Trudie's little sister, Lizzi, were clearly also very fond of him. He had remained in contact with Trudie after they had completed their studies and he had continued to visit whenever he had been in Vienna on business. He and Trudie had enjoyed some memorable evenings at the *Burgtheater* and the *Staatsoper*. He was looking forward to seeing her again, curious about her. Would she be as unchanged as ever or had the events which had overtaken the Jews of Vienna also left their mark on her?

He knocked firmly, three times, as instructed. A small elegant figure, wearing the attire of a domestic servant and beaming vivaciously, opened the door.

"Dr Lewy, I presume?"

"Dr Berger, I presume," replied Harry, raising his hat and bowing deeply in mock ceremony. "*Küss die Hand, gnädige Frau*," he added, putting on his broadest Viennese accent, "I kiss your hand, gracious lady, what a pleasure to see you!"

Trudie chortled with amusement at Harry's feigned chivalry. It was the first time since she had arrived in England the previous August that she had been greeted in the traditional manner of the city of her birth.

• • •

The evening passed quickly. Trudie was required to be on duty from six in the morning so after two hours exchanging news and memories, Harry rose to bid her farewell in the same ceremonial manner with which he had greeted her, followed by a short embrace. He stepped out of the warm kitchen into the cool springtime air, retracing his footsteps to the bus-stop where he had alighted, from where he would then walk at least as far as Paddington.

Striding purposefully through the quiet streets Harry reflected on the evening. It had been the happiest two hours he had known in a long time. In Trudie's improbable new domain as mistress of the kitchen, they had laughed, joked and reminisced at the hectic pace so typical of all encounters with her. He would save the bus fare and walk. He felt almost content and at peace with the world.

Despite everything that had happened in recent months and her drastically altered circumstances, Trudie retained that dynamism, that *joie de vivre* Harry had always loved and admired in her. She had adapted remarkably well to the role of kitchen maid, for which she was totally unsuited by skill, training and temperament. She had quickly confessed that the novelty had worn off. She told him she had heard a rumour that there might be vacancies for women to become teachers if war broke out with conscription being introduced. She quite liked the idea of teaching. Harry had laughed at the suggestion, reminding her of her notorious impatience and intolerance of other people's shortcomings. She had had to agree. Being a schoolmistress might not be the most obvious career, she confessed, but one thing was certain, she, Dr Berger, was not destined to spend her life as a domestic servant of the wealthy. Laughing loudly, she had declared that a fine Viennese lady like herself had no ambition to be London's best scullery maid. They had parted on the best of terms.

Harry looked forward to seeing her again whenever her employers permitted her time off, which was rare. He enjoyed her company, but their relationship had changed from those heady days when for a time they had been inseparable.

Much as he liked her, there would be no going back. For all her lust for life, her wit and brilliance, her almost irresistibly mischievous smile, Harry had no appetite to rekindle the intensity of their previous relationship. He had changed, had become more circumspect, introspective, less spontaneous and more anxious. They shared the common fate of refugees in a foreign land but nothing more.

•••

It was late when he finally arrived back at Edith Road and slipped silently into the house. A dim light from under the door to Mrs Parker's flat illuminated the hallway sufficiently for him to find his way to the stairs.

"Night, Dr Lewy," came Mrs Parker's voice from behind the door.

Does that woman never sleep? Harry asked himself as he climbed to his cold, bare room on the second floor, searching deeply in his pocket for a shilling for the electricity meter.

May – June 1939

Harry's life as a refugee in London had become a multiplicity of paradoxes.

He was free. The sense of imminent terror of his final months in Czechoslovakia had dissipated yet he could not completely shrug off the dull mood of oppression which accompanied him day and night. There were no immediate physical threats, no danger of being arbitrarily arrested in the street and dragged off to a forced labour camp, no officially sanctioned hostility, he reminded himself. Here policemen smiled benignly and saluted when approached and when they were asked for street directions. Harry found this English eccentricity reassuring. He no longer needed to look cautiously over his shoulder or speak in hushed tones if he chanced to find himself in a conversation with a stranger in a queue or on a bus. He was grateful for all these tiny changes in his daily life. They constituted freedom, yet he was unable to savour its taste to the full. In his thoughts hung the heavy shadow of what might happen if war did indeed break out, as now seemed inevitable. And a pitiless longing never left him, to be reunited with his parents and brother and above all, with his former more joyful, happier self, with a life whose purpose and direction had once made some sense to him but now had no higher purpose than survival.

No work or occupation filled the empty hours, yet he seemed constantly busy. In theory he had time on his hands but he never quite managed to complete what he had set out to do on any particular day and this frustrated him. Was this a question of using time efficiently or was it that he found it hard to apply himself, to concentrate on anything substantial? A tenacious lassitude which limited his ability to do anything, had overtaken him. He busied himself with writing letters 'home' to his parents, unsure whether they would ever reach their destination and he waited in vain for news of Arthur. Correspondence with contacts in Belfast about a possible job in the linen industry, something for which he felt he was eminently qualified, was getting him nowhere. Routine requirements such as reporting at the local police station consumed the best part of a morning once a fortnight. By the end of a typical week he was worn out. He walked everywhere and had lost weight but he derived little satisfaction from knowing he was probably fitter than he had been in the years of his previously largely sedentary existence. Despite being overwhelmed by fatigue, he did not sleep well, waking each morning unrefreshed after another restless night. When he asked himself what he had actually accomplished by all the effort of the week, his mind went blank. He was existing, nothing more.

He wrote letters assiduously, consuming precious money on paper, ink, envelopes and postage stamps. Every Monday and Friday he would dispatch a letter to his parents in Dvůr Králové as they waited for clearance to travel through Germany to England. Only occasionally did a reply drop through the letter box in Edith Road. Harry could not conceal his pleasure at receiving the letters, despite the figurehead which heralded an hour of reading and re-reading the few precious words which brought him re-assurance and worry in equal measure. Plans for his parents' departure were progressing steadily if slowly but at every twist and turn obstacles seemed to be thrown up to which Max alluded obliquely. Were these guarded letters being steamed opened and read by those whose allegiance was to the face on the stamp? Probably. Almost certainly. He ensured his own letters were bland, purged of any detail which could compromise his parents if read by prying eyes, as he knew they were, if the stories he heard at Lyons were to be believed.

•••

It was a crisp bright day when, once again, he embarked on the trek from his room in West Kensington to Bloomsbury for a meeting with a representative from the National Council for Civil Liberties. The organisation had offered to help Harry with appeals on behalf of his close friend, Willy, still trapped in the Protectorate and desperate to obtain a visa to come to England. The most important first step was to find a sponsor to put up the necessary £100. Harry had known Willy since childhood. It was his duty, he felt, to do what he could to get his friend to safety. He wrote to the various addresses, gleaned from his visit to Bloomsbury, stressing how skilled, versatile and accomplished his friend was. He approached the task with alacrity, daring to hope he could achieve something but soon he was filled with doubt about the prospects of success. A Monsieur Bernheim in Paris, a contact he had been given at the Corner House, might, in exchange for a small fee, be able to obtain a visa for Willy. He would be as safe there as in England and Willy was at least as competent in French as in English.

Everyone at the Lyons Corner House knew someone, a friend or family member, desperate to reach sanctuary. Since the start of April the authorities had restricted entry to the United Kingdom. It had become much harder to help those left behind. Finding sponsors for penniless refugees was a thankless task.

His first stop that morning was the post office on North End Road, a few minutes' walk from Edith Road.

"Good morning, Dr Lewy," greeted a cheerful voice which belonged to the previously sharp-tongued post mistress. In the short time since his arrival in West London, the post office, along with Marco's and Paolo's café, had become his most frequent destination. The warm greeting this morning was unexpected.

"Another letter for the Protectorate, is it?" she enquired, "you do write a lot, don't you?", she said, with a coy smile, "is it for a lady friend perhaps?" Harry was taken aback. To what did he owe this sudden not entirely welcome familiarity?

"No, not today," he replied as he raised his hat briefly in greeting. "I've got one for France, two for Belfast and one for the United States."

She took the letters and glanced at them, noticing the addresses. "Oh, Paris, it must be lovely there, from all I've heard."

"It is," said Harry without further comment.

He was beginning to warm to Miss Morgan, as he had discovered the post-mistress was called. She might be about his age or perhaps a few years younger, dark-haired, diminutive, with sparkling, lively eyes. Her family, she had told him, had moved to London in search of work from South Wales during the Depression. She also told him that she wanted to train as a nurse, but she was pleased to have found this job, at least for the time being. After their first rather frosty exchange, she had become friendlier. She now obviously regarded Harry as one of her regulars, as she put it.

Harry smiled vaguely but declined to be drawn into a protracted conversation about Paris. Yes, he thought, it was beautiful at this time of year, strolling in the Tuileries with the trees in leaf or acting out a rôle as the young *flâneur* along the banks of the Seine. He recalled with amusement the hours spent sitting on a bench in the Jardin du Luxembourg, ostensibly engrossed in a book but in reality observing the endless procession of stylish young women who caught his eye as they sauntered by. He had felt truly free then.

Harry had things to do. He paid for the stamps, thanked Miss Morgan, wished her a pleasant day and left, once again raising his hat as he left.

•••

Harry enjoyed his walks through the great city. As the weather that morning was fine, he had set out earlier than usual, taking the route through Hyde Park. He had been lucky. For a change there had been no queue at the post office. The few words exchanged with Miss Morgan had not detained him for more than a few moments. His appointment was not until midday. He had time.

He chose a bench already in the sunshine and positioned himself carefully in the middle, denying space to any other potential user. That morning, for no particular reason, he did not want to become engaged in yet another aimless conversation with a complete stranger. So, taking off his hat and placing it beside him to his left and his briefcase to his right, he stretched his legs, made himself comfortable and lit a cigarette, his first of the day. London was peaceful. The noise of the traffic barely penetrated this far into the park and the children who later in the day would play games of tag or hopscotch and fill the air with their shouts and laughter, were at school. He was alone with his thoughts.

Miss Morgan appeared unusually forward this morning, he thought, but in one thing at least, she was not wrong; Paris was a city of romance, at least in popular imagination and never more so than at this time of year. But what about London? Was London equally capable of such charm or was this great mercantile metropolis devoid of romantic possibilities? Miss Morgan, after the initial prickly encounter, proved to be friendly and helpful. Her question about the potential recipient of his letters had momentarily thrown him; was she prying or just being chatty? He wasn't sure. Harry allowed himself a brief speculative chuckle. She was pretty and lively. How might she respond if he invited her to join him on one of his walks through the parks on her day off? Before he could pursue the thought, he was distracted by a family of noisy ducks as it made its way towards him from the nearby Serpentine.

•••

He lit another cigarette. His determination to economise on his consumption of tobacco to reflect his diminished circumstances was not going well. He had smoked since his early student days in Vienna. It was not just socially acceptable but seen as stylish and sophisticated. As he recalled, all the women he knew smoked. His father habitually concluded every meal with a cigar. His own cigarette case was his constant companion, his most precious possession. Neither style nor sophistication were now the reason for his growing consumption of tobacco. The long slow satisfaction which came from inhalation provided a brief calm to which he looked forward at ever-shortening intervals. In Prague the moment Mrs Fischlová handed over the packet of cigarettes she had procured for him was the highlight of the day. Now, short of funds, he had to make every penny go further. He would try to manage on one or two fewer each day. It would be an effort. Uncertain whether he had the energy or will power, he was determined to try.

Another squadron of Serpentine ducks waddled past. The warm spring sunshine induced a passing feeling of well-being. He glanced at his watch. He was killing time. His thoughts drifted back to the anxious weeks before he had fled from Prague. What, he wondered, had become of Otto Heller or of Heinz? Was Mrs Fischlová still receiving guests? It had been a happy stroke of fortune to bump into Helly of all people. What was happening to her and Paul now? Were they too trying to get away? Had they been placed on one of the notorious lists he had heard about, lists of people in whom the Nazi authorities took a sinister interest? He could not imagine why and hoped that they were not in immediate danger.

•••

Memories of meeting Helly in Trautenau in 1932 flooded into his mind. She had been a schoolgirl when he had last seen her before setting off to Vienna and Italy on his studies. The person he invited to join him on the dance floor that evening was, as he remarked to her, quite the grown-up young lady. As the jazz orchestra played a long moody set he was overwhelmed by her graceful beauty and the intelligence of her conversation. For her part, as she later told him, she was flattered by his interest and attentiveness. Harry had never danced with someone quite like Helly before. Although just sixteen, she led him around the floor with startling confidence and style. They had danced a relatively sedate waltz, then a foxtrot and then the Charleston. When the orchestra struck up a dramatic tango, Helly had thrown herself into the dance with passion. Harry felt exhilarated by her verve and her daring as she drove him through the dance. Other dancers on the floor stood to one side to watch. She felt very adult on that occasion, she confided to him later. Harry was different from the other boys she knew at school and who, from time to time, paid her court. Helly had been excellent company; she could be challenging and independent, but he loved her enquiring mind and was constantly surprised by the breadth of her interests and the depth of her insights. She might still be at school, but he felt she was someone special. And she was beautiful. They both looked forward eagerly to their excursions into the mountains, on skis in winter and hiking in summer.

Did I love her? The question remained unanswered.

Harry inhaled deeply and closed his eyes for a few seconds. Was he being sentimental, he asked himself; what was it about her that had seemed so remarkable, so different? He tried to recapture those months when they had spent many happy hours together and which now belonged to a distant age of innocence. Yes, maybe he was being sentimental, perhaps, but so what, and yes, she was special.

•••

His mood darkened, the more he reflected on everything that had happened since then. Was he surrendering to morose self-pity? He did not care much for the answer. The burgeoning relationship, in which he had invested such hope, had come to naught. He bitterly regretted his own foolishness in engineering the row with Helly which led to their separation. He knew on reflection that he had been pompous and self-important about a triviality. His clumsy attempts to align his unspoken aspirations and her overt ambitions had ended in disaster. All this he now understood with great clarity.

Their parting had not been without some acrimony. Contact had then ceased until the chance encounter in Prague in March. Their meeting had belatedly drawn some of the sting from their breakup, an unspoken reconciliation of sorts. She still occupied a space in his mind and in his innermost feelings but Helly too was now part of his past.

∙ ∙ ∙

He stubbed out the butt of the cigarette on the gravel and resolved not to smoke another one until at least two in the afternoon. He would then set himself another target and see if he could eke out an additional hour of abstinence. He had not intended to spend the morning reviewing his life but his vivid recollection of how much his relationship with Helly had once meant to him forced him into confronting the reality of his own present loneliness.

∙ ∙ ∙

A short walk away, if he were so minded, he could immerse himself in the noise and aimless chatter of the Lyons Corner House. Men, many of his age and background, congregated there every day, exchanged news, offered advice, shared misery, wild hopes and profound despair. They talked obsessively about the state of the world, an impotent reflection of their inability to do anything to shape their own destinies. If Harry wanted conversation and male company to assuage his loneliness, it was readily available in unlimited quantity on the Tottenham Court Road and all for the price of a cup of tea and a warmly buttered toasted teacake.

The place had a distinct character which he had learned to navigate. At one end sat the serious chess players who, between carefully plotting moves of self-proclaimed genius, discussed the philosophical dimensions of their situation. Around another table clustered various Marxists gathered in conspiratorial huddles, planning world revolution whilst scouring the newspapers, in English, Yiddish, French or German, for significant items of news. Elsewhere the Zionists had set up camp, discussing how to reach Palestine and evade the British determination to prevent them from entering the forbidden land. In a corner to the rear hovered a group of unsavoury looking figures deep in shady business talk. Yet another table was poring over musical scores, interspersing their earnest conversation with short melodious bursts of song. A Viennese string quartet, no doubt. Nearby was a table colonised by former lawyers who were always locked in earnest debate. A thick pall of cigarette smoke hung over the customers of the Corner House, amidst general shabbiness.

All were to a greater or lesser extent down on their luck, careworn and disoriented, struggling to hold onto shreds of previous existences. The effect was to generate an immense din, occasionally punctuated by a burst of screeching laughter, loud exclamations of surprise or anger or sometimes even hysterical wailing. They were all drifting unmoored from the anchors of their previous lives. Harry accepted that whether he liked the idea or not, that included him. He too was adrift. He needed to find a niche which suited him. None did. He was growing accustomed to a solitary life without attachments or obligations. The life of a refugee.

Cumulus clouds scudded by, briefly obscuring the sun and bringing a sudden chill to the bench where he was sitting. He had gradually descended into a sombre frame of mind as he sat gazing at nothing in particular, lost in thought.

•••

"Morning, sir, everything all right then?" Harry was startled to see two large policemen standing in front of him. He had not noticed them approach. "Pleasant weather for this time of year," said the younger of the two.

"Yes, very fine," replied Harry formulaically, not sure if he should stand up. He remained seated.

"Waiting for anyone in particular?" enquired the other officer.

"No," answered Harry, discomfited by this impromptu interrogation, "just enjoying the sunshine." He looked down at the two cigarette butts lying in the gravel at his feet which suggested he had been sitting at this spot for a while.

"Are you German by any chance, sir?" persisted the first policeman who had spoken. "The accent, sir, if I'm not mistaken, it's German, isn't it?"

"I'm from Czechoslovakia, not Germany," explained Harry, "I'm a refugee here."

"I see. And where do you live now, sir?"

"Edith Road, Number 67. London W14," Harry answered mechanically. "My landlady is Mrs Parker."

He knew that the name of his landlady would mean nothing but he had been given the tip by someone at the Corner House that this additional detail helped reassure the authorities that he was not a vagrant.

"Righto," replied the officer. "Mind how you go. Good morning." The bobbies followed the path down towards the water's edge and the ducks.

•••

Harry had had several harmless encounters with the police since arriving in London. If they were suspicious of him, it was not obvious. Invariably courteous, these enquiries, he accepted, were simply routine. He had not been asked for any proof of identity or further details. There had been nothing threatening or hostile about the two officers. They had been impeccably polite, had called him 'sir' at least three times and, objectively speaking, the exchange could not have been more relaxed. Nothing suggested that they had treated him any differently from any other citizen who happened to be taking the air in Hyde Park that morning. They had not even asked him his name. Despite this, the encounter put Harry on edge. He was an outsider who did not belong here. He was coming to terms with his alien status, knowing he would always have to explain himself, justify his presence in their city, give reasons for his very existence. How exhausting it was always to have to explain himself!

He told himself that he had been swept along by events far beyond his control. He had no work, no home, no family around him, no country, no money or possessions, no girlfriend or wife and worst of all, no prospects. He had been reduced to nothing. Everything had been taken from him. Was he now losing his mind as well? Only a few months ago all this would have been unimaginable. He had become nobody.

•••

Harry glanced at his watch. Overcoming his lethargy, he made his way to the nearby Corner House, pushed open the door and penetrated the fug of smoke mixed with the unmistakable odour of sweat, unwashed clothes and bodies. He sought out the sole unoccupied table in a dark corner away from the entrance, sat down, took off his hat and placed it in front of him. He exchanged perfunctory greetings with the occupants of the neighbouring table, whom he did not recognise and who were speaking Hungarian. He avoided conversation and from his vantage point cast a glance around the busy room.

"You ordered yet, darling?" asked the waitress who, he recollected, had recently brought him the note from Trudie.

"Just a cup of tea, please," he replied.

"Anything with it, teacake, sandwich, whatever you fancy?"

"A couple of biscuits, please."

"Chocolate or plain?"

"Plain will be fine, thank you." He paid immediately.

He again noticed one of the sleazier characters who inhabited the rear portion of the café, a thin, unshaven man in a brownish ill-fitting suit. Only the other day he had advertised himself loudly with the grimmest of laughs and an unmistakable, broad Viennese accent, which Harry found vulgar, as a "purveyor of the finest Veronal sleeping pills to the finest of Europe's wandering Jews." Whether he was genuinely in illegal business or just hawking a savage gallows humour, the announcement had been greeted by total silence. Everyone knew someone who had taken that path and was no longer there.

The waitress brought him his tea and two dry looking biscuits. Everywhere around him were sad faces. The mood was down beat. Harry had no energy on this particular morning to seek out any fellow refugee for company. He stared into his tea, alone and absorbed in his thoughts.

Others have done it. Isn't it time to put an end to all this? It can't be that difficult. The thought came from nowhere, ambushing Harry without warning.

Would anyone miss me? he dared to ask himself, would anyone really notice? Or care, if Dr Harry Lewy had simply ceased to exist?

And how precisely would I do it?

Despite his inner agitation, he sat rigidly still, immobilised and fascinated by the terrible train of thought now taking shape.

He imagined a newspaper report, though unsure in what language, something along the lines of 'Man Takes Own Life'. A non-story. One of many such occurrences.

"Would I really have the courage?" he said aloud.

His musing came to an abrupt end, confronted by the brutality of the question. In truth, he did not know if he could ever go through with such an act, but he was shocked by the violence of what he had been turning over in his mind. Harry shuddered, unsure how serious these thoughts really were; but the one question remained:

Would anyone even ask what has happened to Dr Lewy? His conclusion disturbed him even more than the question.

And his parents and his missing brother? Could he inflict such pain on them? But then, their fate too hung in the balance. Harry could not find answers to the questions tormenting him. They planned to come to England, to be reunited with him. They needed each other and together they would find a way, make a new home for themselves, at least temporarily.

London seemed filled with people like himself, rejected, bewildered, 'half-people', as he called them, refugees from Central Europe. If he chose to do so, it would not be difficult to seek out company, but most of the time, he held back. A deep loneliness had enveloped him. He had always enjoyed the company of women, but he had no enthusiasm or the confidence to seek out new acquaintances. He had once enjoyed going to the theatre but now, without means nor companions, such diversions no longer attracted him. He missed his parents and worried intensely about them but at the same time nursed an uncomfortable feeling, as if he were revelling in his new independence and freedom. Did he feel guilty about being in London, relatively safe and remote from the daily dangers which surrounded those dearest to him? No, he concluded, nothing he had done merited a sense of guilt, yet nagging doubt persisted. Should he feel guilty that fate had singled him out to be free? Was he too ready to surrender to the impotence of his situation? He could not find any answers, gripped by uncertainty about his own future.

He could not summon the strength to pursue his morbid ruminations any further; he would let the terrible possibility with which he had toyed rest for the time being, rather than pursue the hideous idea towards its conclusion. Inertia would prevail for the present as the least demanding course of action. Harry broke his vow and lit yet another cigarette. As he inhaled, he was trembling, his normally steady hand jittering as he brought the cigarette up to his lips. No-one in the Corner House seemed to notice him, just as they would not notice his absence. The dregs of the tea had long since turned cold. He mopped up the few remaining crumbs on his plate, stood up abruptly, put on his hat and made his way out into the street.

"My God!" he exclaimed, shaking, "what has become of me?"

•••

Glancing at his watch he realised his disturbing reverie had allowed time to slip by. He would need to walk briskly or run or even take a taxi which he could not afford, if he was not to be late for his appointment with the Refugee Committee. Yes, he was lonely, more so than he could ever have imagined possible but he had important things to do. He set off at pace down Tottenham Court Road.

•••

"So, Mr Lewy, it appears you have some news for us," intoned Major Hutton-Dacre. Next to him sat not Mr Ševčik but an elegantly dressed middle-aged lady in a hat, whom the Major introduced as Mrs Vaughan, a volunteer with The Committee and someone who had spent many years in Austria and Czechoslovakia. She knew his homeland well, she informed him.

"Yes", replied Harry, fishing a letter out of the briefcase which accompanied him on every visit to an office.

"May I see?" enquired Mrs Vaughan, holding out a gloved hand in Harry's direction.

"Of course."

"An offer of employment," she read, "from the County Down Weaving Company. Do we know anything about them, Reginald?" she asked, turning to the Major.

"Linen handkerchiefs. Exports," he grunted, "should suit Mr Lewy very well."

Then addressing Harry, he added, " there will be a few checks to complete and then, with any luck, you will be off our books."

"Checks?"

"Well yes. First of all the Labour Exchange over there will have to confirm that there are no British workers available for the vacancy and then the Ministry of Labour can issue you with a work permit." For the first time Harry thought he detected a vague smile.

"How long will that take?"

Mrs Vaughan replied with a shrug of the shoulders, adding, "come now, Mr Lewy, we mustn't be impatient, must we?"

"In the meantime, to tide you over, you can still draw an allowance of two Pounds to cover two weeks. Come back again in a fortnight to update us, please."

Harry retrieved the letter from Mrs Vaughan who had shown it to the Major. He folded it carefully and placed it back in his briefcase. As he was getting up to take his leave, the Major intervened.

"Oh, just one final thing before you go, Mr Lewy. The United States. You were granted permission to remain in this country for three months, if I am not mistaken."

Harry looked at him, dumbstruck. Was this some kind of cruel trick? Just as a hopeful prospect seemed to be dangling in front of him, was he now to be informed that the whole thing was an illusion?

"You were due to leave England after 4th July, in other words by the end of next week."

"Yes," answered Harry very softly. He had slumped back into his chair.

"Have you obtained an entry visa for the USA yet?"

"No. I have been informed that my application is in a queue and will not be considered until July 1940."

"Well, we have good news for you, Mr Lewy. In view of deteriorating relations with Germany and the distinct possibility of war, the Home Office informed The Committee a few days ago that it is extending the grace period for another three months. You can remain in England until October at least."

"Thank you, thank you so much," Harry muttered as much in relief as in gratitude, and as if the decision had been taken by the Major himself.

"Oh, it's a pleasure to be able to be of some assistance," replied the Major, now beaming with satisfaction. "You will need to continue to come to the office as agreed and we will make your allowance available until clearance to travel to Belfast comes through. We trust that is in order."

"Yes, thank you, I am so grateful."

London, late August to early September 1939
What would he tell his parents, whose arrival was now imminent? Would he reveal to them the pain, the isolation and sense of insecurity now engrained in him, gnawing at whatever self-confidence he may once have possessed? Would he relate the constant anxiety he had felt about them and Arthur? He had always believed that his parents would make the journey to safety, shielded by the precious little blue document. But Arthur? The unknown fate of his brother tormented him.

And the anger at his impotence, the days of hopelessness and despair? Would he tell them about the mood in the country as the inevitability of war struck home? The signs were everywhere, the sandbags, men in khaki uniforms, air-raid shelters, gasmasks. They would see that for themselves soon enough.

The newspapers and the wireless were full of preparations for war. Conscription had been introduced; London was changing by the day. Perhaps Hitler would be rapidly defeated. The nightmare would pass. Perhaps there was after all a glimmer of hope. Life would go on. Perhaps.

Would he mention the unpleasant incidents, rare in number, but disturbing and hurtful all the same, when he had been insulted as a German or a foreigner or even as a Jew? Or would he satisfy their questions with bland stories, more like episodes in an adventure? There were certainly plenty of interesting and sometimes amusing episodes, but they were shrewd enough to see through a façade which gave only a merry impression. Everything was temporary. He had long had to rely on charity until finally he had received the invitation to come to Belfast where a job was available. In the end, it would probably be an incoherent mixture and in any case they would have their own preoccupations.

MINNA ca 1937

6.
RE-UNITED

A loudspeaker announced the arrival of the train from Harwich. "Another trainload of poor devils," he overheard a porter saying, "Lord knows where they all come from, but there's plenty of them."

The 'Refugee Train' was coming in on platform five just as he reached Liverpool Street station. He found the platform where the train was spilling its ragged contents of mainly elderly passengers and groups of young children apparently on their own, all bearing the hallmarks of the displaced. The older arrivals looked drained and confused as they struggled with their luggage, searching amongst the waiting crowd for familiar faces of loved ones. Harry hailed his parents and ran towards them as they made their way laboriously along the crowded platform towards the exit. They stood there together locked in a long silent embrace of emotion and relief. All three were crying softly, oblivious to the noise, steam and smoke, the bustle of the station, teeming with Europe's rejected humanity.

•••

MAX ca 1937

Germany had invaded Poland earlier in the day. Britain and France had issued an ultimatum. His parents had evidently not yet heard the news.

It was more than seven months since the three of them had been together, months of tension and fear. In the end, Max's and Minna's British passports had protected them but how changed they were, Harry thought. His father had shed a few more hairs as well as pounds but it was his mother who had changed more. Still in her early fifties, she looked older. Her complexion was pallid, her face showing the tell-tale signs of the anxiety she had suffered. It was deeply lined, the face of an old woman. The gentle ever-present smile, even when she was angry or upset, had completely disappeared. She never used to stoop like that. They appeared sad, ill, beaten down. There was relief but no elation in the reunion they had so long yearned for. Here on the forecourt of this busy English station they spoke in guarded whispers, every few seconds casting furtive glances to the left and right of their son, careful not to be overheard or perhaps uneasy about speaking German in a public place. The habits they had had to learn would not be easily cast aside.

As he had done when he had greeted them on their arrival in Dvůr Králové almost a year previously in not dissimilar circumstances,

Harry suggested a revivifying coffee and a bite to eat. There was a Lyons Corner House across the road from the station. English coffee or a white-bread cheese sandwich were not a match for what he would have offered them in Prague or Vienna, let alone in provincial Trautenau, but it would do. They found a table near the window.

"Any news of Arthur?" Harry asked, unable to wait for his parents to give him any news.

"The last we heard, he was somewhere in the Black Sea area. He hadn't got papers for Palestine but he's trying all the same. The British turned him down flat but it seems there are ways, illegally, if you are desperate or determined enough."

"Let's hope," said Harry, "they can't keep everybody out. They've got nowhere to go." He paused. "Nothing more, that's it?"

"No, we have nothing else to tell you. We waited each day for news, a postcard, a letter, a telegram," said Max, "but we got nothing. The postal services in Romania are not very reliable."

"He'll write as soon as he can," added Minna unconvincingly.

"Yes," added Max, "we wrote to him, *poste restante*, in Constanza, telling him we were leaving, and giving your address here in London."

"I've heard nothing," Harry replied flatly, before continuing, " and our house?"

"Property of the Reich," replied Max, "they passed a new law in May making the confiscation officially permanent."

"I thought it was British property."

"So did I but that didn't impress the Nazis. I managed to speak to someone at the Consulate in Prague. Said he would do what he could but that relations with the Germans were getting very difficult and he didn't want to rock the boat."

"And what about the container? You wrote that you had managed to retrieve a lot of things from the house?"

"Container number 231 is sitting in Mr Georg Hammerschlag's yard in Dvůr Králové, awaiting dispatch. It should arrive in Tilbury from Hamburg in the next few days," replied his father. Harry detected a note of scepticism in his father's voice, but he did not pursue the matter.

"Did anything come through from your friends in Ireland?" he continued.

"We've got an invitation to come to Belfast," Max answered, "there are some good people there."

"And I have the prospect of a job," Harry added.

"Now," said Minna, changing the subject, "tell us all about London."

"Later," replied Harry, "there are lots of things to sort out first. I'll tell you everything later."

•••

It was five months to the day since Harry himself had stepped out of Liverpool Street station, alone in his new world. Now reunited with his parents, he embraced them with profound relief.

"Thank God we're together," said Minna, gently stroking her son's cheek with an unaccustomed public show of affection.

So much had happened so rapidly in the intervening months as Europe slid inexorably towards war. Despite everything, were there not some grounds for hope? Surely, opined Max, the might of the British Empire would crush Nazi Germany. Perhaps the Lewy family's stay in England would not last so long after all. Harry detected a flicker of Max's old optimism and faith in the Empire of which he was a proud but tiny fragment. For his part Harry was gloomier about what lay ahead.

Settled around the little table, his mother wanted to know about Harry's time in London, as if she was asking him to recount a series of holiday adventures. Or tales, suitably sanitised, of his stay as a student in Paris. His mind raced over all that had happened since his arrival in England on the last day of March.

Harry took his parents to a small, cheap but clean boarding house in Cromwell Road just around the corner from his lodgings. There they could recover some of their strength before continuing the journey to Belfast. Sheer exhaustion and relief helped them to sleep soundly on their first night in England, but the remainder of the weekend was dominated by the brooding imminence of war. London was all barrage balloons, trenches in Hyde Park and signs indicating the location of air-raid shelters. London was steeling itself.

Anxiety had accompanied Max and Minna too long now for them to attempt to conceal their feelings from their son. Like everyone else on that fateful Sunday, they soon knew of the announcement at nine o'clock in the morning of Chamberlain's ultimatum and the subsequent confirmation, in the most sombre tones two hours later, of the declaration of war with Germany. Harry had taken them to *Da Marco*, the Italian café, for breakfast, knowing that they would welcome Marco's skill in making life-giving real coffee. The café, normally animated and noisy with the regular Sunday morning crowd avid to discuss football and politics, had fallen quiet. Chamberlain's voice came over the wireless, positioned prominently next to the bar. When he had finished a lengthy silence ensured before subdued conversation resumed.

A second war with Germany in their lifetime. No-one there misunderstood the awful significance of these events. Max had said, almost happily, that Germany would be defeated, crushed by the might of the Empire, probably within months. Minna, ashen faced, was thinking of Arthur.

London, Monday 25 September 1939
The London Midland Scottish evening train pulled slowly out of Euston Station, billowing clouds of steam and smoke.

On the platform Harry could see handkerchiefs being waved and tears being mopped from parental eyes. The evacuation of children from the capital, a certain immediate target for aerial bombing in the event of war, had begun on the last day of August. Huddles of children, some sad, some excited, clutching small suitcases and precious possessions, name tags like luggage labels attached to their coats to identify them, clambered onto the train destined for the Lancashire coast. Harry occupied a corner seat in a third-class compartment. Opposite him sat Max and Minna, unaccustomed until recently to anything other than first class. The accumulation of events had left its mark. Max had lost his former confidence verging on ebullience; Minna, always anxious, even in good times, seemed frail. The occasional streaks of light grey hair had turned to a full head of white hair on her once handsome face. Never ostentatious in their prosperity, Max and Minna now looked like the impoverished refugees they had become, although Max shaved carefully and polished his shoes with a ferocious passion every morning as if to emphasise his continuing respectability. Harry assumed that everyone could see the reality embodied in this elderly couple, carrying all their possessions in two suitcases.

There had been final preparations on Monday morning before they made their way across London to Euston station. He took his leave of Mrs Parker. She had been good to him throughout his stay and now prepared some provisions for the journey for the three of them. Normally so punctilious in all financial matters as she accounted painstakingly for every penny, she had refused point-blank to accept payment for what she called just a little snack to keep them going. Harry wanted to insist but Mrs Parker had been resolute to the point that Harry feared offending her if he refused her kindness. He thanked her profusely, grateful for her generosity. If time permitted, he had wanted to call by the post office to bid farewell to Miss Morgan but in the end everything had been a rush. He would send her a postcard from Belfast. That would please her. Harry expected the journey to be arduous for Max and Minna. The sailing from Heysham was not until after midnight and they would not dock in Belfast before eight in the morning, always assuming the Irish Sea was calm for the crossing.

...

The train was full. Most carriages had been taken by groups of evacuee children who were shed like clusters of parcels at various points on the route, the further they travelled from the capital. The additional unscheduled stops meant that the train did not arrive in Heysham until an hour later than planned, entailing a later arrival in Belfast. Harry hoped that the arrangements he had managed to organise for them to be met at the docks would not go awry as a result of the delay. He had written to contacts in Belfast, giving details of their planned arrival. Despite receiving no reply he assumed that everything was in order. This degree of uncertainty, which once might have given rise to great anxiety, had now become perfectly manageable, he mused.

Once on board the Duke of Rothesay, Harry found the two-berth cabin he had reserved at the last moment for his parents. It was an inside cabin with two bunk beds but without a porthole and any other frills. It would, of necessity, suffice. There was a strong smell of disinfectant. The previous crossing to Heysham had been rough and perhaps the last occupants of the cabin had suffered from seasickness. A smooth journey across the Irish Sea would be a blessing. He himself would spend the crossing in the lounge in order to save money. He had been told there were always seats available and that it was not at all uncomfortable. After attending to his parents and assuring them multiple times that he was quite content to sleep upstairs in the lounge, he made his way to the upper deck. Outside on the deck the air was sharp. Leaning on the wooden railing, he tasted the salty breeze that was getting up and allowed himself one final cigarette before settling indoors for the crossing. A few men standing at the bar drinking slowly from large glasses of dark beer were talking loudly. Harry found a quiet corner as far away as possible from the bar and made himself comfortable. He promptly fell soundly asleep. The sea was calm and the crossing uneventful.

Belfast Tuesday 26 September 1939
Dawn had already broken when Harry awoke feeling unkempt, grubby and unrested. He yearned to relax in a warm bath, a distant prospect at that moment. In the toilets he splashed water on his unshaven face vainly attempting to freshen up. His mouth was dry, the taste sour. He straightened his tie and ran a comb through his thinning hair, endeavouring to restore a semblance of smartness. He was hungry but without appetite and decided to forgo the delights of the small restaurant. He would save a few pennies. Instead, he turned to the last of Mrs Parker's sandwiches and a small corner of homemade cake. It tasted heavenly, he decided. He hoped his parents, still in their tiny cabin, would enjoy their modest breakfast as much.

7.
NEW WORLD

By the time they joined him in the lounge, the Duke of Rothesay was approaching the sheltered waters of Belfast Lough, on both sides of which Harry could see rolling green countryside, gentler to the south, starker and more dramatic to the north. Everything looked calm and peaceful; small, neat farmsteads dotted the landscape and black and white cows were grazing in tidy fields. Along the edge of the coast from time to time a small village came into view; wisps of blueish smoke drifted lazily from orderly rows of chimney pots which crowned the whitewashed cottages. Occasionally they passed a puny boat surrounded by a company of eager hovering gulls as it returned to one of the villages from a night's fishing. It looked so very different, idyllic, unthreatening. What kind of place is this? Harry asked himself.

It would be an hour before they docked so Minna returned to the cabin. Max suggested to Harry that they go out on deck and watch as the boat carefully navigated the channel at the entrance to the harbour. This was a journey he had made several times in more benign circumstances. In those days he had not even considered anything less than first-class travel. He had always taken a single berth cabin with a porthole and room service and arrived in the city ready for the day ahead. He would check into the Grand Central Hotel in Royal Avenue, the glory of late-Victorian Belfast architecture and widely reputed to be the finest hotel in all Ireland. There he would run a bath, change into a fresh suit and enjoy a light sea-food lunch in one of the hotel's celebrated restaurants before his first appointment. He reminisced to Harry who had heard his father's Belfast stories many times.

"Belfast," Max told him in the manner of an official guide, "is a mighty industrial city, one of the most important of the British Empire. As you arrive at the mouth of the River Lagan, you see the gantries and cranes of the Harland and Wolff shipyards. To the west, in the shadow of the hills are the great mills which manufacture the world-famous Irish Linen. That's where Mackies have their engineering factory and that's where the weaving machines for the linen mills in Trautenau come from."

Harry was no longer listening to the familiar account, part travelogue, part geography lesson. His mind was on more immediate matters. The boat eased its way carefully alongside Donegall Quay where long sheds lined the waterfront. By the time the boat had docked and tied up and the wooden gangways had been put in place for the passengers to disembark, the three of them had joined the other passengers thronging on the deck, impatient now to be ashore. The doors to the arrivals shed were thrown back; an expectant noisy crowd was waiting to welcome the newcomers. Goods and luggage were unloaded. There was no indication of a country already at war to disturb the morning routine of the arrival of the boat from Heysham.

To one side stood two pairs of men in dark-green police uniforms and flat caps, observing the scene. Everything seemed normal on a busy working day.

Harry scanned the crowd looking for the familiar face he hoped was somewhere in its midst. Then he spotted her, a small slim woman, frantically waving a red handkerchief. She was flanked by two male figures, one a solidly built man in a loose-fitting suit, the other, an imposing figure in formal dress and a top hat. As Harry and his parents, clutching their precious cases, carefully made their way down to the quayside, the young woman surged forward to greet them.

"Harry!" she exclaimed, throwing her arms around his neck and holding him tight. "Thank God you're here. It's wonderful to see you!"

"Edith," replied Harry, "we are so happy to see you. Thank you for coming to meet us."

Harry unwound himself slowly from her embrace; she held out her hand to greet his parents. "Mr Lewy, Mrs Lewy, It's marvellous to see you again. It's been such a long time. I hope you have had a trouble-free journey." She paused, adding after a moment, "and welcome to Belfast."

"And it's a pleasure to see you again, Miss Geduldiger," replied Max somewhat formally, "we're all a long way from home. The journey here was fine, thank you. It's such a pleasure to see a familiar face." Smiling, Max added, "and I hope you are keeping well."

"Yes, we are well. We have nothing to complain about," answered Edith, "our life is very different here. I am sure you will get used to it." She paused before continuing, "I am so glad you're both safe and well. These are terrible times."

Max returned Edith's smile but said nothing further. He felt no need to expand on the privations and difficulties of their travels from their land-locked homeland in Central Europe to this island in the Atlantic Ocean.

Turning back to Harry, Edith continued: "How are you? You must be worn out."

"Well, we're just relieved to be here, Edith," he replied somewhat wearily, "and to be together again."

"Any news of Arthur?" she enquired.

Before he could reply, the solidly built man, who had pressed his way to the front of the crowd, intervened to introduce himself.

"Kohner," he announced, holding out his hand, "Franz Kohner. I am Edith's husband. We are so glad you are here." The important-looking gentleman in the top hat now appeared. Harry observed that in their excitement and delight, they had been speaking German. Franz now switched into English.

"And this is Mr Barney Hurwitz, the president of Belfast's Jewish community, he's here to welcome you officially and to assist you," explained Franz.

A deep voice with an unfamiliar accent now spoke slowly and rather formally, addressing Max.

"Welcome to Belfast and Northern Ireland, Mr Lewy. We, that is to say the Belfast Jewish Refugee Committee, have made arrangements for your accommodation. Everything is in hand. You will be safe here. There is nothing to worry about, you can be sure of that," he said, adding, "my chauffeur will bring your luggage to the car which is waiting outside. Please come this way!"

"We are most grateful," replied Max, bewildered by the suddenness of developments. He had not given much thought to what might await them when they finally got to their destination.

Harry had told him he was in touch with people in Belfast but had said nothing about Edith. The last time Max and Minna had seen her was several years before in Trautenau, when she was still Edith Geduldiger. The Geduldigers, also in the linen business, had invited the Lewys for dinner more than once in their new ultra-modern house, the epitome of successful, entrepreneurial prosperity, mixed with the best of modern design. The Lewy and the Geduldiger families were longstanding friends. Edith, three years younger than Harry, was present. They had all enjoyed the most convivial of evenings. Edith and Harry had been fond of each other. Harry had suspected an ulterior motive behind his inclusion in the invitation to dinner that went beyond the opportunity to admire the magnificent new Geduldiger residence. Shortly afterwards he learned that Edith was to be married to a lawyer from Brüx.

"What a coincidence!" exclaimed Minna, now speaking for the first time, "here we are, far away in a foreign country and who's the first person we meet, a girl from Trautenau! How is that possible? Maybe it's a good sign."

Harry was relieved at her comment. It was the first positive remark his mother had made for as long as he could remember. She was not generally given to believing in omens, good or bad. Perhaps, he hoped, her gloomy mood was lifting. Mr Hurwitz intervened to escort them to his car. A Bentley, Harry observed. Mr Hurwitz was clearly someone of significance.

The gleaming limousine made its way swiftly through the dingy narrow streets surrounding the docks, under trolleybus wires and across tramlines and gradually uphill into a leafier district. Harry stared out of the window at row upon row of terraced houses, some grander than others. He was struck by the proliferation of churches and in the near distance, the dramatic outline of the hills which formed a backdrop to the city.

The car drew to a halt a short time afterwards in an unremarkable looking street of terraced houses.

"This is Glantane Street," Mr Hurwitz announced. "The Refugee Committee has rented a few houses in this neighbourhood. We have taken a first floor flat for you at No 52."

Harry looked up at a large bay window. The houses formed a terrace of once elegant Victorian properties, now beginning to show early signs of neglect. They could do with a lick of paint. Harry was reminded of Edith Road. The smell of coal fires hung in the damp morning air although it was still only September, the plumes of smoke floating upwards towards the line of hills. Down the street the sun was glinting on the battleship grey water of Belfast Lough; beyond, in the distance lay the green fields he had noticed as the boat had approached the great port. He had never been anywhere like this.

Mr Hurwitz continued in a business-like, authoritative tone, a brisk man in a hurry, clearly with no time for small talk.

"The flat is furnished. Simply but adequately for your needs. There are two bedrooms, a living room, a kitchen and a bathroom. You will require coins for the gas and electricity meters. Otherwise, in the interim, the community will meet your expenses until you have had a chance to settle in."

Standing on the pavement surrounded by their luggage Max and Minna gazed around them. From the day they had been forced to flee from Trautenau, they had learned to adjust to their new and changing status.

They had concentrated all their efforts for so long on getting away, getting out of the trap which held them and finding somewhere they might feel safe and secure. They had never really thought seriously about arrival and had made no plans for a place they might need to call home for the foreseeable future.

Now, after lengthy train journeys and sea crossings, reality was beginning to sink in. This was not a temporary adjustment but the start of a new life in a new world. As a young man Max had found the experience of exchanging his familiar surroundings on the Baltic for the Veldt of Transvaal exhilarating. Now in his sixties, he felt nothing but crushing exhaustion. From where would he summon the strength to start again? Minna too felt bewildered. Her English was limited; the new surroundings were brutally unfamiliar. How could she even begin to set up a household here?

Harry shared his parents' anxieties but made a conscious effort to conceal them. For the moment, he would display positive enthusiasm even as he dwelt on the problem of finding a job which would enable him to support them. How long was Mr Hurwitz's 'interim'? As if divining their thoughts, Mr Hurwitz resumed his stream of vital information.

"You have everything you will need close by. Just up there on the Antrim Road are the shops. There is a baker and a kosher butcher. If you walk down the Antrim Road towards the city centre, you will find the *shul*. It's about twenty-five minutes on foot, just off Carlisle Circus. There's a trolleybus service for when you go into town."

"When you have found your feet," he continued, now addressing Harry, "we will have to talk about finding you some sort of gainful employment. I understand you know about textiles. But that's for another day."

"Actually I have an offer of employment from the County Down Weaving Company," interjected Harry, "perhaps you have heard of them?"

"Indeed I have," replied Mr Hurwitz non-committally.

"You are most kind, we are truly grateful," Max repeated. He had visited the synagogue once in the 1920s while on a business visit but he could not begin to locate it from Mr Hurwitz's description. They would manage.

"Oh, it's the least we can do," Mr Hurwitz said airily before Harry could respond further to the remark about finding a job. "I hope we will see you all regularly at *shul*. You will be most welcome. We have had several additions of your sort to our congregation recently."

"Thank you," said Harry. What sort did Mr Hurwitz have in mind? Was he talking about other recently arrived refugees from Nazism? Did he really mean the growing number of penniless people thrown on the charity of the Belfast Hebrew Congregation and its Refugee Committee? Probably. The Lewys were that sort of people now.

Mr Hurwitz took out a watch on a chain from a waistcoat pocket and glanced at it.

"Goodness me, is that the time? I must be gone. There's a day's work to be done. A man has to work for a living, you know. Here's my card. Contact me if you need anything. Don't hesitate!"

Mr Hurwitz signalled his imminent departure to his chauffeur standing nearby, who rapidly stubbed out his cigarette on the pavement, adjusted his peaked cap and opened the door of the limousine to usher Mr Hurwitz to his seat. As he got in, Edith and Franz appeared from around the corner. They had taken the trolleybus.

"Let's get you up the stairs to your new home," said Edith, "and then we can tell you all about this place."

As Mr Hurwitz had explained, the door was unlocked. They stepped inside and surveyed the scene, bare walls, a shabby rug concealing most of the wooden floorboards, a cold hearth and chimney breast for a coal fire, the most basic furniture, a meter in a corner into which they would have to feed coins, a vague cooking smell emanating from the rear yard, mingling with the smell of smoke.

"Refugee rooms," murmured Minna. No-one dissented.

Minna lifted the smaller of two bags onto the table and took out a wooden framed photograph. Looking round the room for a suitable location, she finally placed it on the chimney breast above the hearth where it would conceal the signs of damp on the peeling brown-striped wallpaper.

"Do you remember this, Max?"

"Yes, the Stadtpark in Trautenau," he said.

"Yes, the last time we were all together, all four of us. February 1938. Harry's twenty-ninth birthday."

"How solemn we look, how respectable! But we were happy then, perhaps for the last time," Max's fading voice said wistfully.

Harry stepped forward to look more closely at the photograph. He and Arthur looked youthful and carefree; how his parents had aged in the intervening eighteen months.

Harry turned away from the hearth and gazed around the room. It had a certain ugly familiarity but it did not look nor feel like home.

Belfast, Friday 10 November 1939

A gale was blowing as the rain started to fall on a cold grey morning in early November. The smell of the peaty smoke from the hearths of rows of the narrow terraced streets running down to the docks filled the small apartment in Glantane Street, now the home of the Lewy family. As they peered out of their first-floor window it was Cavehill and not the Giant Mountains which dominated the skyline to the north. How unfamiliar it seemed. The day before had been Minna's birthday. She had baked a cake with a few raisins and poppyseed and they had assembled around the kitchen table for a subdued celebration. It was a year to the day since Max had returned empty-handed from his expedition to Prague to be greeted by the news of the pogroms across the Reich. Despite the disappointment and futility of that day, he could never have imagined them taking refuge on an island off the mainland of continental Europe. Still, there was a synagogue here within walking distance, intact, spared the rampage of destruction from which they had escaped. It was not as magnificent as their former synagogue; the dark wooden pews were sombre and austere by comparison with the building in Rinnelstrasse. But the Lewy family had been made welcome in their new surroundings and there were indeed a few others, also a long way from their former homes, whose experiences matched their own. A tiny community of the displaced.

Amidst the harsh Northern Irish accents, the universality of the Hebrew liturgy was re-assuring and comforting to Max and Minna. They had met one or two other families who had fled from Vienna and Breslau and with whom they could converse in German to the evident disapproval of other members of the congregation, who considered it unpatriotic. Harry even caught snatches of Yiddish which he could not fully understand. He was assiduous in his determination to speak only in English. Had his parents also been given a little blue book of useful advice when they had first arrived? It would take time for them to fit in here.

The kosher butchers nearby provided a chance encounter from time to time with a fellow newcomer in this cold city, someone with whom snippets of news and worries could be shared. The established local Jewish community on the one hand seemed to keep its distance but on the other organised much practical and material support. In their own abrupt way, people were kind and helpful. News from the former homeland was hard to come by and from Arthur not a word. Max and Minna had become accustomed to their frugal lives in the hope that Harry would ultimately find a job and a less precarious existence for them all.

•••

Harry followed the instructions, the key parts of which were written in capital letters on the piece of paper he was clutching. He read and re-read the text quietly to himself.

> 'From the south side behind the CITY HALL follow LINENHALL STREET. Towards the T-junction with ORMEAU AVENUE on your right is No 37. The COUNTY DOWN WEAVING COMPANY is on the first floor. Go up the stairs to the glass door. Ask for Mr HILLIS, he should be expecting you'.

Harry was early for his appointment at midday. From a doorway he contemplated the scene as he drew slowly on his Gallahers cigarette. The local brand was strong and rough. The red-brick public swimming baths across the road, the small terrace houses in the narrow streets leading off the tree-lined avenue, and the grander institutional buildings along Linenhall Street leading up to the City Hall were alien to him. The smell of town gas lingered everywhere in the air, mixed with the tang from the sea and the piercing cries of the gulls, attracted by easy pickings at the nearby market. He was wearing his smarter suit, of the two he possessed, as well as his widely travelled leather coat, hat, scarf and gloves, as instructed by his mother. He hoped he looked smart and would make a good impression.

•••

Standing on this gloomy street corner, Harry wondered if he was at last on the threshold of a new life. What did it mean to be a refugee? He had had months to ponder the question from the night when he had been forced to abandon his former life in such dramatic circumstances. He marvelled ironically at his own adaptability.

What once might have seemed to him the stuff of second-rate fiction had become his everyday normality. He went nowhere without the papers and documents necessary to prove he still had the right to exist, to breathe the same air as everyone else. He had learned to have a small case always at the ready, lest time ran out for more careful preparations. He had also learned to be distrustful, to be deferential when dealing with officialdom, not to get into arguments with those in authority over him, no matter how lowly that person was in someone else's hierarchy. He had come to accept that he had few rights, which could, in any event, be peremptorily removed. He had grown accustomed to separation, from friends, from his brother and for a long period, from his parents. He barely recognised the person he had once been.

Now he and his parents were safely reunited in a cramped flat in North Belfast which bore every resemblance to the shabby rooms they had had learned to call home for almost a year. He existed with great care in a world in which every item of expenditure, down to individual cigarettes, was carefully costed. He had learned to be grateful for even the smallest expressions of kindness which came his way. He was accustomed to living in a kind of twilight world, the pending tray of his life.

Would he return one day to his home? This question troubled him deeply. Where would home be for him now? Yes, he once loved the mountains which formed the beautiful backdrop to Trautenau and yes, he had loved the thrill of skiing on the fresh snow every winter and yes, he had been comfortable in the little town where he was born and had grown up. And yes, he had for a brief while enjoyed his bachelor existence in his comfortable flat in Reichenberg. Yet, as he now looked back, had he ever truly belonged there? Too young to have ever been an Austrian, he was not truly Czech either. He had never been a German Sudetenlander, although the Sudetenland was where he lived. He shared a common language with his classmates, but it had been the same former classmates who, years later, had burned his family's place of worship to the ground, driven him out and stolen his family's house and property. It had been his fellow students in Vienna who humiliated and tormented the city's Jews when *Anschluss* cast them adrift. He could not shed his mother tongue, but neither could he identify with what Germanness now meant in the eyes of the world. To what would he want to return? His mind was empty in response to all these questions.

Perhaps to Czechoslovakia, if there was once again to be such a country. He had always struggled with the language, had little knowledge of Czech culture and traditions and even less affection for them. If he was honest, they did not hold much interest for him either in comparison to the excitement that he had felt in France and Italy. The antagonism of the Czechs towards Jews, particularly Jews like himself from a German background, had degenerated into open hostility and personal danger in his final few weeks in Prague. That experience had snuffed out any notion of genuine affiliation to Czechoslovakia. He no longer belonged there.

Perhaps to Palestine? In no sense could Harry see himself 'returning' to Palestine. The idealism of *Aliyah* had never appealed. Fleeing there in search of shelter, perhaps, but returning, no. That strand of Zionism which proclaimed a right of return to the biblical land of his supposed ancestors held no attraction and no meaning. No pioneer spirit suffused his thinking, despite the passionate urging of Edith's husband, who had become a friend and would-be mentor. He felt no connection to the Jews of antiquity. He recalled standing under the ancient Arch of Titus in Rome, gazing in wonder at the frieze of the Roman Emperor's subjugation of the Jews in 70AD. It was fascinating as a structure but as a representation of people like him, with whom he could identify, Harry had looked and felt nothing. The Jews expelled from Spain in 1492 were a fact in history, much like the victims of the Kishinev Pogrom. He felt no visceral fear of the Cossacks. Perhaps with the passage of time, he mused, he would become part of the patriotically British local Jewish community which staunchly proclaimed its proud allegiance to the Empire. But that was not how he felt on this cold November morning. Where, if anywhere, did he belong?

The Zionism which proclaimed a homeland for all Jews, where they would be safe from centuries of persecution, perhaps, after all, that did now hold some faint attraction. Years before, he had been dismissive of the idea of European Jews like himself abandoning their comfortable assimilated lives in Vienna, Berlin or Paris to toil in the fields and make the desert bloom, as the Zionist pamphlets, reprising Isaiah, put it. But now he could see there might be some sense in the idea. Perhaps, after all, he was part of a greater continuity of transience; that it had been the historical fate of Jews, from time immemorial, to be uprooted, to be driven from their homes and to have to find a new foothold in some unknown corner of the world. Perhaps he was connected to this long history, whether he had previously wished to acknowledge it or not. Palestine? Would he really ever belong there? His new acquaintance, Franz Kohner, who had set up a centre outside Belfast to prepare and train young Jews for agricultural work in the Promised Land, tried relentlessly to recruit him. Did it appeal to him? Harry was not convinced but perhaps his younger brother was right. Perhaps the dream of a Jewish homeland was not so misguided. The yearning for permanence was real and for the first time in his life made vague sense. Perhaps, one day. But as matters stood, Harry, a citizen of nowhere, had his mind on other more immediate things.

•••

He glanced at his watch. Twelve noon. He surveyed the grimy building where he had his appointment.

"Well, let's see," he muttered to himself.

He climbed the wooden stairs to the glass door and knocked. He had rehearsed his words.

"Come in," summoned a woman's voice. Harry entered to behold a smiling, friendly-looking woman in glasses; office tables stacked with papers, an opaque window which could do with cleaning. The unmistakable smell of tobacco.

"I have come to see Mr Hillis, please," he said, removing his hat.

"Over here," boomed a man's voice from the far end of the room.

Harry walked across the office towards the voice. Its owner, a balding, thick-set man in short sleeves, was engrossed in a ledger and did not look up at the visitor for some time. Harry was left standing awkwardly in front of the desk.

"And you are Mr Lewy, I presume?" he finally enquired without making eye contact.

"Yes, Dr Lewy, Dr Harry Lewy, sir. I understand you have a position vacant."

"Yes, we have," said Mr Hillis, "One of our chaps is off to the Navy. Got to keep the business going, somehow. War effort and all that." He rummaged through the pile of papers on the desk.

"I have a letter here somewhere about you. Ah, yes. You are 'warmly recommended' it says here. 'Reliable. Intelligent. Quite knowledgeable about textiles. A hard worker'."

There was a pause. Mr Hillis raised his head from the documents in front of him and looked Harry up and down, scrutinising every detail thoroughly.

"That's you, is it, Mr Lewy?"

"Yes sir."

"When can you start?"

"I can start immediately, sir, if that would be acceptable to you," Harry replied, wondering whether he sounded too obsequious or just polite. He had been advised that the British always addressed their superiors or even strangers as 'sir'.

"Perfect. Nine o'clock. Monday morning. We can discuss your duties and remuneration then."

"Thank you very much, sir, I am most grateful to you."

"Well, that's that. Monday 13th. Remember to bring all your documents with you. Don't forget the one with the RUC stamp on it. Oh, and we don't need any of that fancy doctor stuff, it'll be plain Mr Lewy here."

WHAT HAPPENED NEXT

The former Lewy family home at Reichstrasse 25, now Polská 25, in 2016

Harry Lewy (1909-1991) settled in Northern Ireland and worked in the textile industry for the remainder of his life. After the end of the war Harry searched for and found Helly's name on a Red Cross list of survivors. In 1947 he became a naturalised British citizen and holder of a British passport. A few months later he returned briefly to Czechoslovakia and on 16 June 1947 married Helly Herrmann, née Katz in Prague's historic Town Hall. He never visited the country again.

Wedding, Prague Town Hall, 16 June 1947

In 1949, after Max had died and with the birth of a first child imminent, he changed the family name by Deed Poll to Lewis. He and Helly had two sons, born in 1949 and 1954. It was Harry's unconditional love and support for Helly which sustained her through the painful years of her recovery and rehabilitation. His final act of devotion to Helly was to type out on file paper the manuscript of her memoir which was to become *A Time to Speak*. He died peacefully in 1991 at the age of 82 on the eve of their 44th wedding anniversary. Her memoir was published the following year.

Max Lewy (1874-1949) spent the rest of his life in Belfast in much reduced circumstances and died in 1949 after a period of illness. The former family home in Trautenau / Trutnov, confiscated after 1938 by the Nazis and after the Liberation in 1945 by the government of Czechoslovakia, was never returned to the Lewy family.

Minna (1887-1974) remained in Belfast. She never talked about her lost son, Arthur, but lit a *Yahrzeit* candle each year in his and Max's memory. She died in 1974.

Arthur (1911-1944) made his way illegally to Palestine. He never saw his brother and parents again and died there of typhoid in 1944 at the age of 33.

Helly (1916-2009) – Helly Katz survived the Holocaust but lost her mother, her first husband, Paul Herrmann, and many family members. In 1947 she married her childhood friend, Harry Lewy, and emigrated to Belfast where she lived and worked for the rest of her life. Physically and mentally scarred by her experiences, she gradually reconstructed her life and became a celebrated innovative choreographer and teacher. In 1992 her memoir, *A Time to Speak* (Helen Lewis, Blackstaff) was published to great acclaim. It has been translated into Czech, Italian and Portuguese. Her contribution to the Arts was recognised through honorary doctorates from the University of Ulster and The Queen's University, Belfast. In 2001 she was awarded the Medal of the Foreign Ministry of the Czech Republic. In 2002 she was appointed a Member of the British Empire. She died on 31 December 2009.

In 2018 a blue plaque was unveiled in her memory at the Crescent Arts Centre in Belfast, of which she was the patron, and in 2023 an authoritative dance biography, *Shadows behind the Dance* by Maddy Tongue, was published by The Irish Pages Press. In June 2023 a memorial stone, a *Stolperstein*, was unveiled in Prague outside the block of flats where she and her husband had lived until their deportation in August 1942.

Harry ca 1946

AFTERWORD

I have for a long time wanted to tell something of the story of Dr Harry Lewy. It is a story unlikely to find its way into any history book, but in its own way is emblematic of the experiences of many refugees, driven from once secure homes, to make a new life for themselves in a strange world.

Leon Harry Lewy was born in 1909 into a German speaking Jewish family in Trautenau, then in the northern border region of the Austro-Hungarian Empire. His parents originated in what is present-day Lithuania, at that time the borderlands of the German and Russian Empires. The area where he grew up came to be known as the Sudetenland and was incorporated into the newly created country of Czechoslovakia at the end of the Great War. Overwhelmingly Bohemian and German by cultural history, language and tradition, the region became an international flashpoint and focus of Hitler's expansionist ambitions for his German and Aryan race. After the Munich Agreement in September 1938, the small and well-established Jewish communities of the Sudetenland fell victim to

Nazi persecution. Those who could, fled for their lives. That was the fate of Dr Harry Lewy.

I never met Dr Harry Lewy, but I did know Mr Harry Lewis, as he came to be known, for over 40 years. He was my father. His story is remarkably unremarkable. He was one of many thousands of refugees, each of whom had their own past and their own story. I have tried to capture this mere fleeting fragment of a bigger picture.

Harry Lewy found shelter, acceptance and peace in the country in which he sought refuge. He was fortunate. Although in his own mind he always remained an outsider, he was able to rebuild a shattered existence.

The plight of the refugee has not gone away despite international conventions and obligations to which many nations have agreed but then often honour in the breach. War, persecution, poverty and despair continue to create a seemingly unending number of displaced people, whose existence somewhere in the world has become completely untenable.

Now, as in the past, when the Lewys made their perilous journey in search of sanctuary, the refugee's existence is precarious. Rarely welcomed with open arms, they are often seen as a problem or even a threat. Labelled as refugees or asylum seekers or migrants, these people are made into something alien and other. The result is to strip the most vulnerable of their rights, their dignity, their individual identity and humanity. They cease to be people like us.

This story attempts to reclaim part of one refugee's story, his identity and humanity.

Michael Lewis

January 2022 to September 2024

NOTES

Page 10

The **Sudetenland** was the name given to the region to the north and west of Czechoslovakia, bordering Germany. Its population was predominantly German-speaking. After Hitler came to power in Germany in 1933 agitation for greater autonomy for the area developed rapidly, stoked by Nazi demands for annexation. By 1938 this had become a fully-blown international crisis with the imminent prospect of war.

In late September a conference was held in Munich. France and the United Kingdom were formally allies of Czechoslovakia and guarantors of its independence. The conference was attended by Mussolini and Hitler, Neville Chamberlain for the United Kingdom and Edouard Daladier for France.

On 30 September 1938 the four participants signed an agreement, forcing Czechoslovakia to cede the Sudeten region to Germany with immediate effect. The Sudetenland became part of the German

Reich. Czechoslovakia was not represented at the conference which decided on its dismemberment.

"Heim ins Reich" – " back home into the Reich" - the rallying slogan of the Sudeten German Party, expressing its demand to be integrated into Hitler's Third Reich.

Gut yom tov – a traditional Yiddish greeting of good wishes on festive occasions.

Page 11

Rosh Hashanah – the Jewish New Year. In Jewish practice, the start of a festival or Holy Day begins at sunset on the evening before.

Yom Kippur – the Day of Atonement. The most solemn and holy day in the Jewish calendar, during which Jews fast from dusk on the eve of Yom Kippur until the following evening. It begins 10 days after the New Year.

Page 14

Shofar – a biblical trumpet-like instrument made from a ram's horn and sounded at the conclusion of Yom Kippur and other religious occasions.

Page 15

Konrad Henlein (1898-1945) – political agitator and leader of the Sudeten German Party, he joined the Nazi Party and the SS in 1938. He committed suicide in American captivity on 10 May 1945

"Juda verrecke!" – Judah Perish! Death to the Jews, a favourite Nazi slogan.

Page 16

Vienna On 12 March 1938 Germany invaded and annexed Austria. The Viennese turned on their Jewish neighbours in an explosion of public violence and destruction, arrests and imprisonment in concentration camps.

Anschluss – the takeover of Austria on 12 March 1938 and its incorporation into the Grossdeutsches Reich, the Great German Empire.

Page 17

Memel – today Klaipeda, Lithuania.

New Year 5699. In the Jewish calendar, 25 September 1938 marked the beginning of the year 5699.

Page 18

Freikorps – para-military groups, often of armed former soldiers.

Page 20

Beneš – Edvard Beneš (1884-1948) – President of Czechoslovakia from 1935-1938, leader of the Czechoslovak government-in-exile during World War Two and president again until his death in 1948.

Kishinev – today Chisinau in Moldova, the scene of repeated pogroms against Jews. In 1903 47 Jews were massacred in riots and in 1905 another 19 were reported to have been killed. The pogroms attracted world-wide attention.

Page 23

Kol Nidrei - the evening service which opens the Day of Atonement – Yom Kippur – begins with a declaration annulling any vows made under duress. In popular usage the entire service goes by the name, Kol Nidrei.

Page 34

Passover Seder, " **Mah nishtanah, ha-laylah ha-zeh, mi-kol ha-leylot?** *Why is this night different from all other nights?*" – The Passover or Pesach, which takes place in the spring, celebrates the deliverance from Egypt. The evening service or Seder traditionally takes place over a meal around the family dining table. Children play a central role. The youngest child present asks what is special about this particular evening as a prelude to the retelling of the story of how God guided Moses to lead the People of Israel across the parting waves of the Red Sea to safety.

Pesach – Passover.

Page 35

Haggadah – the story of the Passover is told in the Haggadah. The purpose of the Seder is to transmit the history of the deliverance from generation to generation as told in this special book.

bouquinistes – bookstalls along the Seine in Paris.

Drumont – Edouard Drumont (1844-1917), a notorious French anti-Semitic writer, propagandist and publisher who achieved great popularity in the late nineteenth and early twentieth centuries for the violence of his attacks on Jews.

Dreyfus – Alfred Dreyfus (1859-1935), a French Jewish army officer, wrongly accused and sentenced to imprisonment on Devil's Island as a traitor. Following a long campaign, which deeply divided France, Dreyfus was found innocent and rehabilitated.

Page 36

Lueger – Karl Lueger (1844-1910) - mayor of Vienna, famous for modernising the city but also for his populist anti-Semitism.

TG Masaryk – Tomas Garrigue Masaryk (1850 - 1937), philosopher, politician, Czech nationalist, champion of democracy and first president of Czechoslovakia.

Hilsner Affair – Leopold Hilsner (1876-1928), a vagrant and Jew was accused in 1899 of the ritual murder of a Christian girl in order to use her blood for making unleavened matzos bread at Passover. TG Masaryk took up the case and defended Hilsner who was found guilty and sentenced to death. The sentence was commuted by the Emperor to life imprisonment. Although rare, "blood libel" cases persisted in Europe well into the 20th century.

Page 43

Czechoslovakia or Czecho-Slovakia

After the Munich agreement on 30 September 1938, the original Czechoslovakia of the First Republic ceased to exist with the forced secession of the Sudetenland to Nazi Germany. This represented 38% of the historic Czech lands of Bohemia and Moravia. This was followed by further territorial losses to Hungary and Poland; Slovakia became an autonomous region. What remained was known as the Second Republic; the revised country acquired a hyphen and became Czecho-Slovakia. This too ceased to exist on 15 March 1939 when Germany occupied the rump of Czechoslovakia. The Second Republic lasted 169 days.

Page 46

Prager Tagblatt

An influential German language daily newspaper, (1876-1939), widely read in liberal and democratic circles.

Incident in Paris

On 7 November 1938 a German Diplomat, Ernst vom Rath was shot in Paris by Herschel Grynszpan, a young Jewish refugee. Grynszpan had learnt that his parents had been deported from Germany to Poland. Vom Rath died on 9 November. His death triggered a co-ordinated orgy of destruction, murder and arrests across the whole Reich, including in the Sudetenland. These events came to be known as *Kristallnacht* or the Night of Broken Glass, nowadays referred to as the *Reichspogromnacht* or Night of the Reich Pogrom.

Page 58

Girls' Gymnasium – Girls' Grammar School.

Page 60

Geheime Staatspolizei, Dienststelle Trautenau – State Secret Police, Section Trautenau – The local Gestapo.

Page 66

Aliyah originally an ancient term meaning "going up to Jerusalem", it was adopted by Zionism as meaning going to or returning to the Holy Land or Palestine.

Page 67

The Riesengebirge the Schneekoppe

The Giant Mountains immediately to the north of Trautenau formed the border with Germany, now Poland. The Schneekoppe at 1602 metres is the highest point.

Page 85

Emil Hácha (1872-1945). A Czech lawyer, he became president of the Second Republic in November 1938 and oversaw the decline of what remained of Czechoslovakia after Munich from a democratic to an authoritarian state.

Page 86

Joseph Roth (1894-1939) Austrian Jewish journalist and novelist; his most popular novel, *Radetzky March* (1932), was a family saga set against the background of the decline of the Austro-Hungarian Empire.

Page 92

Heine (1797-1856), Heinrich Heine, German poet and writer, born into a Jewish family but converted to Protestantism in 1825. The reference here is to a verse in *"Deutschland ein Wintermärchen"*. Heine's sharp satirical wit and mordant criticism as well as his Jewish origins made him a particular target for Nazi hatred.

Page 99

Zweig (1881-1942) Stefan Zweig, Austrian Jewish author who enjoyed world-wide popularity in the 1920s and 30s.

Page 110

Johann Wolfgang von Goethe (1749-1832) and **Friedrich Schiller** (1759-1805), celebrated German poets and playwrights.

Page 122

The British Committee for Refugees from Czechoslovakia (BCRC)

In the aftermath of the Munich Agreement on 30 September 1938 a voluntary non-governmental committee was established to aid those in Czechoslovakia and later the Protectorate deemed to be in the greatest danger from the Nazi authorities. It negotiated with the government to admit those threatened with persecution and provided limited financial support to destitute refugees. Thus the Committee was able to assure the government that the refugees would not be a burden on the British tax-payer. In July 1939 it became the Czechoslovak Refugee Trust (CRT) under government control. It ceased to exist in 1979.

Page 124
'racial'
A three level classification of those at risk was introduced after Munich.

Those deemed as the highest priority for rescue and admission to the UK were political activists such as members of the Social Democratic Party or trade unionists in the former Sudetenland.

The second category covered those who had fled from Nazi Germany after 1933 and Austria after *Anschluss* (see note to page 4) in 1938 and taken refuge in Czechoslovakia. This group included political activists, writers, artists and journalists. A significant proportion were Jews.

The lowest category were Jews who had been living in the Sudetenland. This category was designated as 'racial'. It applied to all those covered by the Nuremberg racial laws and not just those who identified as Jews or who practised their religion. Initially many were regarded as 'economic migrants'.

Page 131
While you are in England: helpful information and guidance for every refugee

On arrival German-speaking Jews were issued with a booklet providing a mixture of useful advice and instructions. Various aid committees had been established from as early as 1933. The Board of Deputies was and is the representative organisation of British Jewry.

Page 192

RUC – Royal Ulster Constabulary – the police force in Northern Ireland at the time.

A NOTE ABOUT CZECHOSLOVAKIA

You will search in vain for Czechoslovakia on a 21st century map of Europe. The country created by the Treaty of Versailles at the end of the Great War in the heart of Central Europe formally dissolved itself in 1993 and ceased to exist. This was not the first time that Czechoslovakia had disappeared from the map in the course of its short existence.

Trautenau, where Harry was born in 1909, was a small industrial town in northeast Bohemia on the edge of the sprawling Austro-Hungarian Empire. As a child he played in the town park at the centre of which stood the memorial to the men of the town who had fallen in the colours of the Austrian Emperor, Franz Josef, at the nearby battle of Königgrätz in combat with the Prussians, during the Austro-Prussian War of 1866.

By the time Harry was 10 the Empire had been dismembered and the new multi-ethnic, multi-lingual state of Czechoslovakia under the leadership of its first president, Tomáš Garrigue Masaryk, had been born. The ancient Czech-speaking lands of Bohemia and Moravia were amalgamated with Slovak-speaking Slovakia. There were sizeable Polish and Hungarian minorities and to the north, west and southwest of the new country, along the border with Bavaria, Saxony and Silesia, lived a German-speaking population of about three million people. These were the Sudeten Germans and the area bore the name Sudetenland.

Trautenau was 95% German by language and culture. In the main cities of Prague and Brno Czechs and Germans lived side-by-side. Jews had also lived in these lands for many centuries; in the course of the 19th century many had gravitated to the towns and cities. Trautenau had a small established Jewish population, part of Czechoslovakia's Jewish minority.

After the Nazis came to power in Germany in 1933 Sudeten agitation for autonomy increased greatly. By 1938 Hitler's unrelenting demands for the German population of the Sudetenland to be fully incorporated into the Reich were accompanied by threats of military force. The developing international crisis appeared to bring Europe to the brink of war. Britain and France, although formally allies of Czechoslovakia, adopted a policy of appeasement and caved in to Hitler, agreeing against the will of Czechoslovakia to consign the Sudetenland to Nazi Germany. The Munich Agreement of 30 September 1938 took immediate effect and signaled the disintegration of the country. By March 1939 Slovakia had broken away and established a fascist Nazi client regime under the cleric, Jozef Tiso. On 15 March the Germans occupied Prague and the rump of Czechoslovakia and set up The Protectorate of Bohemia and Moravia. Independent Czechoslovakia had ceased to exist and endured the longest Nazi occupation of any country until liberation by Soviet and Allied armies in May 1945.

The Czechoslovak Government in Exile returned and the state was re-established. More than 2.5 million Germans were expelled in what we today call "ethnic cleansing". Initially once again a democracy, Czechoslovakia by February 1948 had become the Czech and Slovak Socialist Republic, firmly behind the Iron Curtain and a staunch Stalinist member of the Warsaw Pact. An attempt at liberalisation during the "Prague Spring" of 1968 was brutally repressed by the Soviet Union and its allies.

Communism collapsed with the "Velvet Revolution" of November 1989 but by 1993 the two component parts of the country had decided amicably to go their separate ways. The new countries gained accession to the European Union on 1 May 2004.

Trautenau, now known exclusively by its Czech name, Trutnov, still nestles at the foot of the Giant Mountains. There is no German population nor Jewish community in the town. A sombre plaque marks the ruins of the synagogue destroyed on 9 November 1938. The Lewy family home, however, is still standing where it always was. The address is no longer Reichstrasse 25 but Polská 25. The letterbox still bears the German word for letters, *Briefe*.

Documents

A: LETTER FROM CAPTAIN JOHN TAYLOR

(letter of alien) →

This is to certify that I have known Mr. Max S. Lewy, flax merchant in Trautenau, Czechoslovakia, for seventeen years.

He rendered valuable service in South Africa during the South African War. He has also been of service to British firms in the flax and linen trade. He himself is a naturalized British subject, but his sons have not got British nationality. In view of the help that Mr. Lewy has always shown himself ready to render I should be grateful for any assistance which can properly be shown him.

John W. Taylor
His Majesty's Consul.

British Consulate,
VIENNA.
12th April, 1938.

o t o fotografické vyhotovení souhlasí doslovně s prvopisem sestávajícím o jednom 1/2 archu nez kolků.
Okresní soud ve Dvoře Králové n/L., odd. III.,
dne 19. května 1939.

This letter from HM Consul in Vienna, Captain John Taylor, is dated 12 April 1938, one month after the Anschluss, the annexation of Austria by Nazi Germany but six months before the Munich Agreement. Captain Taylor had known Max Lewy from when he was stationed in Prague in the early 1920s. The letter recognises the precarious position of Harry and Arthur but does not commit the British Government to any course of action.

A hand-written annotation, "father of alien", indicates that Harry must have presented this letter at some point as proof that his father was a British citizen by naturalization.

B: POLICE RECORD for HARRY LEWY

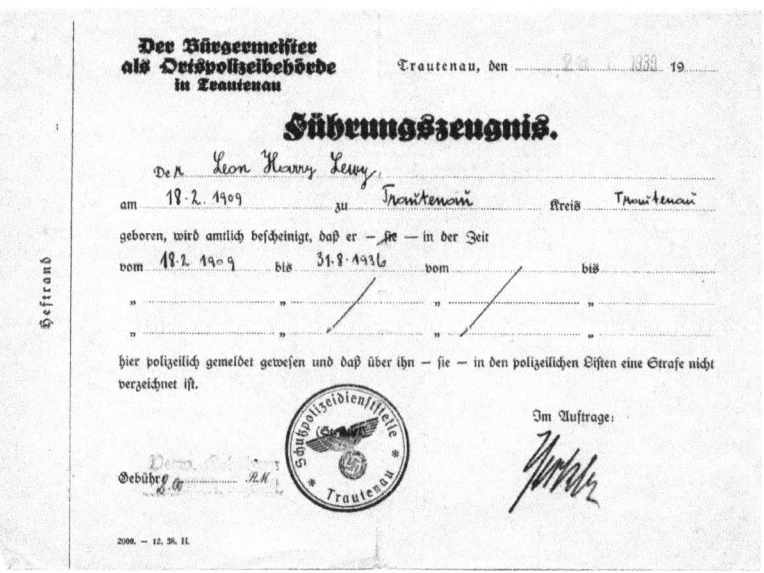

This statement dated 28 January 1939 was issued by the Nazi authorities in Trautenau. It confirms that between the date of Harry's birth and 31 August 1936 he had a clean police record with no criminal offences. After that date Harry was no longer registered in Trautenau but subsequent police records have not survived.

This was one of many documents Harry had to compile in order to be permitted to leave Czechoslovakia.

C: NATIONAL COUNCIL for CIVIL LIBERTIES (NCCL) – LETTER of INTRODUCTION

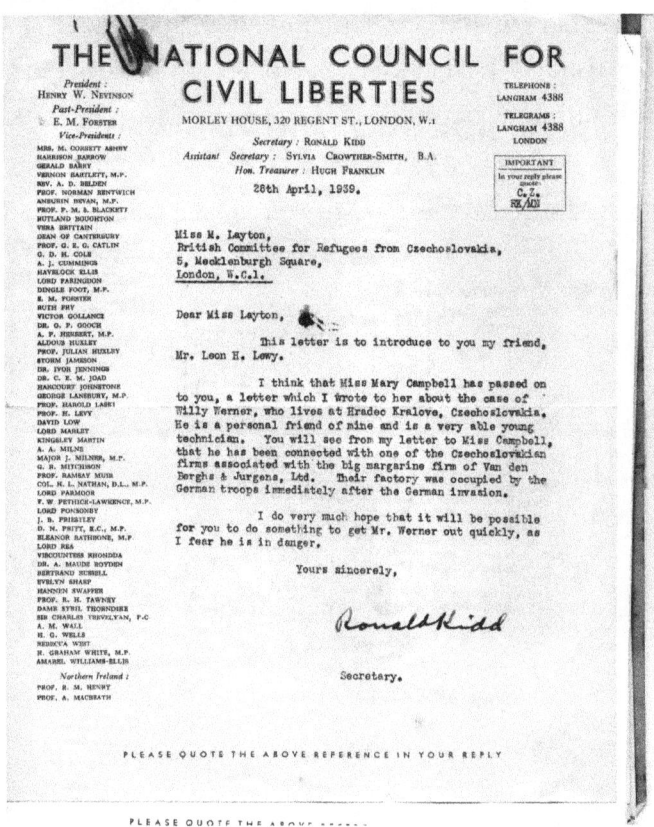

Within days of arriving in England, Harry was making efforts to get his childhood friend, Willi Werner, to safety. This letter from the Secretary of the NCCL, today known as Liberty, to the British Committee for Refugees from Czechoslovakia incorporates a statement from Harry seeking the Committee's support to "get Mr

Werner out quickly as I fear he is in danger". Harry was unsuccessful. He never saw his friend again.

D: RECORD of HARRY'S INTERVIEWS WITH THE BRITISH COMMITTEE for REFUGEES from CZECHOSLOVAKIA (BCRC)

Document courtesy of the National Archives, reference HO294/551/5610

Date of Interview	Report on Interview	Maintenance grant sanctioned
5.4.39 april 18.4.39	[illegible handwriting] food for one week to 12th Apr. He has received £1 from Mrs. Ross. He tries to get work. Food etc. 25sh. Will write to Edinburgh. Has written to American consulate. Father is English.	2/6 15/-
May 8th	Mr. R. wishes to send him for a time to the Gamp. Rev. L. will still make more efforts. I have a rather good impression. one week maint. £1, 5 sh.	
28.VI.39	See note of Dr. Rehfeld. Support 1 week. S.B.	
5.7.39	He already applied for a permit to work with the County Down Weaving Co., Coniston Building, Dublin Road, Belfast, who have offered him a job. He does think there is no chance of his getting a permit unless (a) they raise his salary considerably, (b) they try to prove to the H.O. that they have tried also to fill the post with a British employee but failed. I think he knows Fry in London 2 weeks.	
19.7.39	No reply from firm yet. Have written to enquire. Is confident that he will be taken, as a friend is in a similar position, & he has so many Czech connections. 1 week m. — R.B.	
26.7.39	It seems that he will get a permit almost immediately through the Ministry of Labour. Maintenance for one week. Had to prove his father of British Nationality. DT	
2.8.39	Says that the firm (C.D.W.) have applied for a permit themselves and that he is waiting for the answer. (They applied on July 5th). Mr. Rocker will write to firm. maint. 1 week. DT	
9.8.39	He have written to all Labour Exchanges in Northern Ireland. Result in 10 days. DT	
16.8.39	Nothing further yet. He is in touch with firm who will have immediately permit is through. 1 w/2 RB	
20.9.39	Reckoner wk 3 weeks to Oct 11. RB	

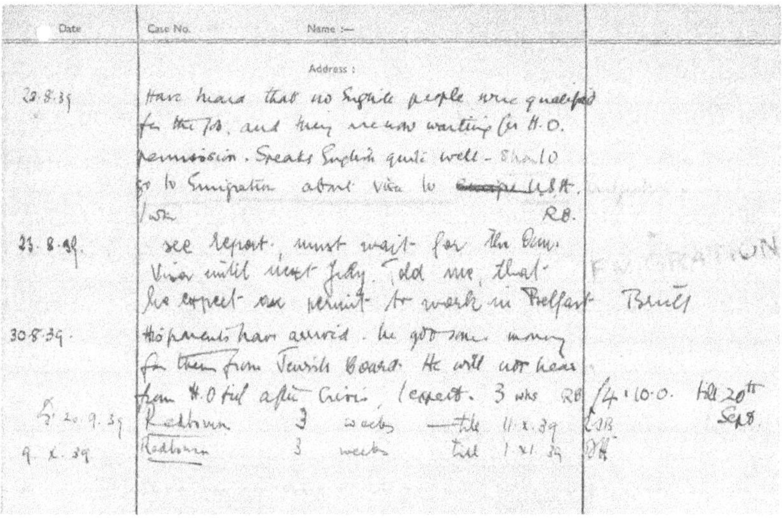

Notes

[Handwritten ledger entries, partially legible:]

Date	Case No.	Name :—
		Address :
20.8.39		Have heard that no English people are qualified for the job, and they are now waiting for H.O. permission. Speaks English quite well — Should go to Emigration about visa to ~~Europe~~ U.S.A. I ask. RB.
23.8.39		see report. must wait for the Dom. Visa until next July. Told me that he expect one permit to work in Belfast. Brutt
30.8.39		His parents have arrived. He got some money for them from Jewish Board. He will not hear from H.O. til after Crisis, I expect 3 wks RB /4·10·0 till 20th Sept.
20.9.39		Redtown 3 weeks ~~till 11.x.39~~ CAB
9.X.39		Redtown 3 weeks till 1.XI.39 DH

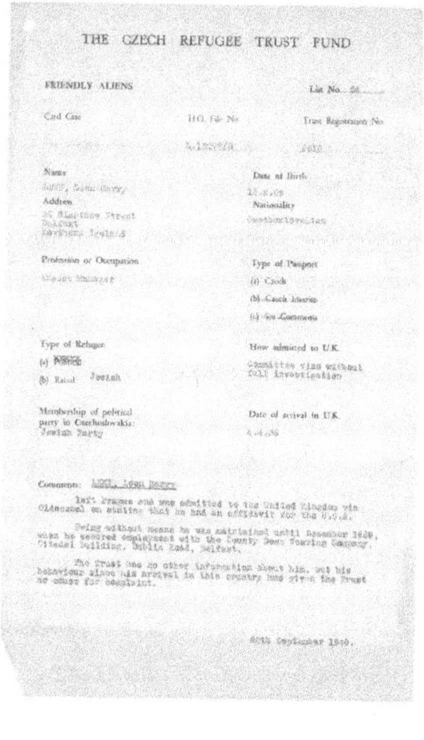

THE CZECH REFUGEE TRUST FUND

FRIENDLY ALIENS   List No. 56

Card Case   H.O. File No.   Trust Registration No.

Name: [illegible]
Date of Birth:
Address: [illegible] Street, Belfast, Northern Ireland
Nationality: Czechoslovakian

Profession or Occupation: [illegible]
Type of Passport:
 (a) Czech
 (b) Czech Interim
 (c) [illegible]

Type of Refugee:
 (a) ~~Political~~
 (b) Racial Jewish

How admitted to U.K.: Committee visa without full investigation

Membership of political party in Czechoslovakia: Jewish Party

Date of arrival in U.K.:

Comments: [illegible]
left Prague and was admitted to the United Kingdom via Oldenzaal on stating that he had an affidavit for the U.S.A.

Being without means he was maintained until December 1939, when he secured employment with the County Down Weaving Company, "Citadel Building, Dublin Road, Belfast.

The Trust has no other information about him, but his behaviour since his arrival in this country has given the Trust no cause for complaint.

30th September 1940.

Between April and Autumn 1939 Harry was required to report regularly to the BCRC, which gave him a meagre living allowance. The Committee also recorded his progress in obtaining a visa to travel to the USA or alternatively gain employment. The printed note BRITISH SUBJECT was added in March 1947, after Harry had been naturalised. This document is held in the National Archives in Kew and sealed until 2030. It was released in 2024 following a Freedom of Information request.

E: WHILE YOU ARE IN ENGLAND

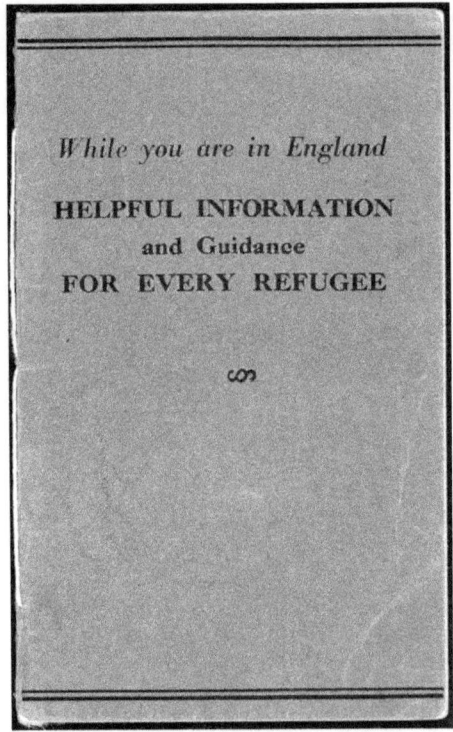

The cover of the booklet, in English and German, issued to refugees arriving in England.

ACKNOWLEDGEMENTS

When in early 2022 I finally began to write down the ideas which had been swirling around my mind for a few years, I wanted simply to tell the story of my father. I did not set out to write a book for publication. The fact that nearly four years later the story has become a book is due to the kindness, patience, encouragement and interest of people I acknowledge here.

Without their support, Flight from Prague, The Making of a Refugee as a book would never have happened.

Over many years my sons, Dan and Ben, have been fascinated by our family history. They were too young to know Harry when he died in 1991, but their sense of family has never diminished. Their probing questions and curiosity have been vital. This story is part of their story and will one day belong to their children and future generations, who may want to know.

To my long-standing close friends Richard Lindley and John Turner, I owe an immense debt. They were the very first people outside our family with whom I shared early versions. Their positive reactions, interrogations, questions and appetite to know more were powerfully affirmative. They were in no doubt that my efforts merited a wider audience and helped me overcome my doubts.

The positive enthusiasm of former colleagues and friends, Julie, Fran, Huw, Mark, Penny, Phil, Sally and Phill, who read various drafts, asked questions, made comments and suggestions were unequivocal in their encouragement that I should seek to see the project through to publication.

It was John Birtwhistle, my friend and neighbour here in Broomhill in Sheffield, who took me in hand. John, a former academic and accomplished published poet and librettist, was unstinting. Over many cups of coffee he analysed, challenged and gently criticised but never deviated from his view that what he was reading was worthwhile. It was John who insisted that "every word must earn its place on the page". If I have proved a poor pupil and fallen short, it is not for lack of effort or perseverance on John's part.

It is nearly 35 years since Harry died. There are few people who still remember him today.

My brother, Robin, has been a key figure in getting the story this far. His ability to recall details of conversations with Harry was crucial to testing the authenticity of the story. It had to satisfy not just his lawyer's scrutiny of fine detail and relevance but also the harder test of finding the truthful tone and gesture. It was Robin's judgment I feared most. His approbation, his comments and advice all counted greatly and my gratitude to him is immense.

Robin took on the task of extracting critical documents from the National Archives in Kew. He also secured the generous agreement of the celebrated Irish poet, Michael Longley, our long-standing family friend and neighbour in Belfast, to include his poem, *A Linen*

Handkerchief, which in eight lines encapsulates the odyssey of my parents.

I am grateful to Martin Hickman and Gaby Monteiro at Canbury Haythorp for the expertise and enthusiasm with which they have brought the raw text to publication. This has taken me into entirely new territory. I am still learning and count myself fortunate to have found in them such a sympathetic team.

It is to my wife, Petra, that I owe the greatest debt. When the urge to tell a story became a compulsion, it was Petra who bore the brunt of this obsession which did not respect occasion or time of day or night. Petra, of course, knew Harry, who had warmly welcomed her, his German daughter-in-law, into the family. It was not always easy for her to live with someone in the grip of a new driving force, constantly wanting to try out a barrage of words, phrases and ideas. When self-doubt took hold, it was Petra who insisted that perseverance was the best way through. What I got in exchange was infinite patience, laced with unflinching but always constructive comment and criticism. Not everything survived and I believe the story is better for the omissions and inclusions she guided with firmness and tact. Without her sustained support, there would have been no book.

A Linen Handkerchief

for Helen Lewis

Northern Bohemia's flax fields and the flax fields
Of Northern Ireland, the linen industry, brought Harry,
Trader in linen handkerchiefs, to Belfast, and then
After Terezín and widowhood and Auschwitz, you,

Odysseus as a girl, your sail a linen handkerchief
On which he embroidered and unpicked hundreds of names
All through the war, but in one corner the flowers
Encircling your name never came undone.

Michael Longley
The Weather in Japan 2000

MICHAEL LEWIS

Michael Lewis was born in 1949 and grew up in Belfast where he went to school. His father, the subject of this book, was a refugee and his mother was a Holocaust survivor. After reading Modern Languages at Oxford, he trained as a teacher at York University. He taught in 4 comprehensive schools in England for 35 years, the last twenty of which were as the headteacher of King Edward VII School in Sheffield. After retirement in 2008, he took on a variety of roles , including as a non legal member of the Employment Tribunals (2010-2024), as a member and sometime chair of the Independent Ethics Panel of South Yorkshire Police (2015-24) and as a member of the Teaching Regulation Agency's professional conduct panel.

In 2009 the University of Sheffield awarded him an honorary Doctor of Letters in recognition of his contribution to education.

He married Petra in 1979 and they have two sons and two grandchildren.

More titles from Canbury Press

100 Immigrants Who Made Britain Great
Inspiring Stories of Talented People
Louis Stewart and Naomi Kenyon
ISBN: 9781914487460

Introduction by Bonnie Greer, the Chicago-born playwright and cultural commentator.

How I Survived a Chinese 'Re-education' Camp
A Uyghur Woman's Story
Gulbahar Haitiwaji
ISBN: 9781912454907

'An intimate, highly sensory self-portrait'
Sunday Telegraph (Five Stars)

Are you an author?

We give writers the opportunity to see their work in print

We specialise in memoir, biography, autobiography and history,

but will consider other factual genres.

haythorp.co.uk

contact@haythorp.co.uk

www.ingramcontent.com/pod-product-compliance
Lightning Source LLC
Chambersburg PA
CBHW031317160426
43196CB00007B/566